My Escape to Freedom

Iron Curtain Memoirs

Book 3

by

Irene Kucholick

Three Kings Publishing

Princeton, Kentucky

Three Kings Publishing
115 Canterbury Court
Princeton, Kentucky 42445

To my Mother and Nadja: without them, us kids would not have survived.

Acknowledgments

With many thanks to my good friend Sam Cooper, who spent much time, helping me greatly with research and general detail work. Also many thanks to Phyllis Hole who helped and worked with me to start this enormous amount of labor and urged me to go on when I wanted to give up. I want to thank my good neighbor Merlin Berry, who gave me many good tips and helped greatly over the last year of writing. Thanks so much to my brothers Hartmut and Claus, (Ortwin died in 1961), who were able to dedicate their time and helped me with many details. But above all, I want to thank my husband, Walter P. Kucholick, who always gave me great encouragement.

BUILDING
1948 - 1952

Being a girl again was an exhilarating kind of self renewal. I was almost nineteen and the pretty dresses and shoes Theresa gave me were a source of real pleasure.

Saturday night dances became the highlight of our social activity. They were held in a once fashionable dance hall and restaurant, nestled in the woods near the town of Adelsberg.

Krista and I walked with my brothers and other friends to this weekend event where we were soon caught up in the pleasure of flirtations, laughter and jolly good fun. I had learned how to dance in West Germany and the boys sure noticed me in my pretty clothes.

The Russian Army of Occupation did not interfere with our weekend dances. Although we knew they were near, and they showed themselves now and then, they stayed in the background. They were more disciplined now and we were getting used to the Russian soldiers. Now, we even saw many Russian girls in uniform.

Some German women, young as well and middle aged, still invited Russians into their homes. There they fraternized, even though it was forbidden to do so. Maybe some of them were in love, but Stalin's army punished such human behavior.

To us the Russian soldiers looked forlorn and poor. Their feet were still wrapped in ragged strips of cloth under boots which they aired in the open windows of their barracks. There they fluttered, grey and dingy, where once German soldiers had kept things so shiny and clean. The khaki color of their Cossack shirts did not hide their dingy look. Their winter coats seemed to all have been made in one size. Shorter soldiers simply cut their coats to a usable length and wore them without a hem, giving an unkempt appearance. They sang lively marching songs though, just as the Germans used to do. We often saw details of about 30 men marching and singing in their unhemmed coats.

By contrast, the Russian officers had better living conditions, better tailored uniforms, more food, more privileges and much more freedom.

Due to the Russian desire for theater and ballet, those forms of recreation were revived at the earliest possible date. Russians flocked to these cultural events. Soldiers were brought to the theaters by the bus loads, though they were not allowed to mingle with the German popularity. Much propaganda was made to support the German-Soviet friendship, for which we had to pay monthly dues. Yet the Soviets and the Germans were not even allowed to say "Hello" and "How do you like the German ballet?"

Tall and beautiful, my cousin, Margo, was a ballet dancer. Her never ending need for silk stockings was the chief reason we saw each other often. As soon as Margo heard that we received a box of silk stockings from Theresa, she came with food to trade for them. On one occasion she came in an old black chauffeured Nazi car, creating much curiosity amongst our neighbors. Out of the car stepped a high Russian officer with much brass and many ribbons on his uniform. He turned around and helped Margo out of the car. She was dressed very fashionablely. The chauffeur, a soldier, was told to wait.

Margo and the Russian officer came into our humble home and seemed to feel comfortable with us. Mama exchanged our silk stockings for foods. We learned that Margo was deeply in love with the Russian officer, but we knew that they would never be allowed to marry. Mama saw nothing but heartbreak in their secret love affair. When they learned the apartment above the horse barn was empty, they used those quarters for their rendezvous. Colonel Boris, as we called him, confiscated furniture to provide for their needs.

Since Colonel Boris's rank exceeded that of the village commandant, nothing was reported. When a car was parked near the barn we knew Margo and her Colonel were there.

In April of 1949 I entered a special prep school in Chemnitz to study for entrance tests in the field of nursing. After completing these tests I appeared before the Board of Examiners in order to enter nursing school.

"When you go in, say very little" coached my teacher, "Just answer 'yes' or 'no' to medical questions, but when they ask you political questions talk at great length. They like talkative people when it comes to politics." I did not understand politics well enough to say much and I felt utterly inadequate for the task.

On that important day, four men sat behind a long, high desk covered with a red cloth that hung nearly to the floor. Two of the examiners, who had self-important expressions on their rugged red skinned faces, were the politicians. The other two, whose faces and manners indicated more discipline, were the medical examiners.

3

The political questions came first. When I could not answer quickly, one of them would bark, "You lost one point there. Hurry it up!"

"How many miles are there in the East German border?"

I did not know how long this hateful border was.

"What kind of government do we have in East Germany?"

I did not know how to explain something so quickly that I did not like. I felt discouraged and we had hardly started. One of the men stood up, towering above me. He looked much taller than an ordinary man. I wanted to talk but I couldn't. I decided to run from the room and turned to leave.

"Come back here! Stand still, Genosse! All right, I will ask you something easier." He looked amused.

"What is the capital of East Germany? Ha ha."

"Berlin."

This was followed by other simple questions. They wanted me to talk about the German-Soviet friendship and whether I would be willing to make donations to this "worthy" cause. I knew I was expected to say "yes."

The medical examiner was courteous but thorough. My head was filled with physiology, anatomy, chemistry and bacteriology. I began to think I'd made it through this part of the examination in good shape. We were given the test results after long hours of anguished waiting.

I passed! Then on to the written tests. Which I also passed. It was exhilarating to succeed in the first steps of my chosen field of work. All that remained was the endless wait for the letter telling me where I could study. It was during this period that Margo came to our home to exchange food and sad news for silk stockings. We sensed a problem since Colonel Boris was not with her.

"Aunt Ella, you know my love for Boris. We cannot marry and I am going to have his child."

Mama was noticeably shocked. I knew mama had always admired Margo, her beauty and grace were as poetry to me.

"Margo, what can I say? I am so sorry." Mama was searching for words. "What will you do?"

"I don't know, Aunt Ella. Here are tickets to the next ballet. Perhaps you and Irene would like to come."

"Could you go to Russia with Colonel Boris?" I asked.

She shook her head. "It would be impossible," she replied. "If the officials knew what was happening they would transfer Boris back to Russia immediately. We would never see each other again. We'll have to keep it a secret as long as possible, then we'll see."

"I wish I could help you Margo." Mama said, and her face looked worried. Margo left with her silk stockings and a great burden in her heart. At that moment I saw the sorrow of illicit love and the anguish it was causing Margo and her mother.

The letter came saying I could attend the Rabenstein School of Nursing in Chemnitz. Rabenstein was considered to be the best and most disciplined school for nursing. Both Mama and I knew that nurses finishing there were always in great demand.

Ortwin, now 16, was attending the technical high school in Chemnitz. His plan was to build motors and "be as good at it as Papa was with radios." Ortwin was taller than me now and looked a little like Papa, with wavy brown hair and blue eyes. He had no more time to work at the farm anymore and this caused a loss of produce.

My classes started and I began the most grueling travel schedule I was ever to endure in my lifetime. Rabenstein Hospital was on the opposite side of Euba and there was no dormitory space available for me at the time. No train schedule could accommodate my need to be in class at eight o'clock each morning. I walked about nine miles in a southerly direction to Gablenz, where I caught a street car. This took me into the central Johannis Square of the city. Here I transferred to another street car out to Siegmar Schoenau. From there a twenty minute walk through Pelzmuehle Park and up a hill put me in class on time each morning.

Following an eight to five class I reversed this long trek to return home each evening. These daily journeys in all kind of weather lasted for almost a year. No one ever seemed to notice how exhausted I was. It was just expected that I would always endure. No one ever thought that I might fail.

Mama would say, "If you are cold, walk faster."

"Think warm thoughts," Hartmut would tease.

I marched on frozen snow and ice, in icy winds, heavy thunderstorms and steady rain. I marched in sunshine and on grey days but there never seemed to be enough sunny days. The last three miles home were the most exhausting part of my day.

Ortwin had the same long trip to Chemnitz but his school was close to the street car line. Hartmut started his training in an agricultural School near Dresden. Hartmut lived at the school and came home on weekends.

Rabenstein Hospital and Nursing School were housed in several large buildings that stood on the crest of a hill and resembled a summer resort, except for the high fence and gate that restricted those who entered or left the grounds. A few smaller buildings, housing, maternity and isolation wards, adjoined a pleasant park where patients and nurses often walked during leisure hours.

Our uniforms were light blue dresses, over which we tied a white apron during working hours or a short cape for street dress. We wore white caps with seven stiff starched pleats. They were not for decoration. We were required to stuff all our hair inside them except for a few curls in front. I remember the heavy starched caps cut my hair off on both sides of my head; the edges were almost as sharp as a knife. My shoes were a delight, comfortable and well fitted for walking. I could never have walked the miles required of me on a daily basis in the poorly fitted military boots. To this day the shape of my feet are not what they would have been if I had always worn well fitting shoes. We were allowed to take baths every day and I felt especially clean in my uniform.

Our studies included pharmacology, chemistry, physiology, anatomy, surgery and neurology. We also studied biology, bacteriology and more. Our instructors were highly qualified doctors and nurses. We studied nutrition and enough mathematics to be able to make our own medicinal solutions. In the pharmacy we were required to smell and taste all medicines so we would know what we were giving patients and so we would avoid making mistakes. We learned the human body inside and out and while we had our little jokes, the emphasis was on learning.

Around the middle of my first year of study, Aunt Martha told us of Margo's tragic death. She danced in the ballet as long as possible, then left the stage to stay at home. Her baby was delivered prematurely with only a midwife present. She died in childbirth, her baby boy living only a few hours. Her lover, the Russian officer, left immediately for Russia. No one in the family ever heard from him again.

Just before spring I was assigned to a dormitory room with three other student nurses. Their roommate had broken the rules and was dismissed from the program. Her leaving was my good fortune--no more walks and rides to and from school each day. I shared a room with Katharina, a Hungarian girl whose father had moved to Brazil after the war. The rest of Katharina's family lived in Germany. Roswita von Warvenstein, whose German parents had to leave a large estate in Poland when borders changed, and Marianne Betzold, a heavyset girl whose parents once owned a farm, were my other two roommates. Now the government owned the farm and Marianne's parents worked there as farmhands. It was the communist way.

We lived under many regulations. Uniforms were worn at all times. My roommates and I never worked in the same ward on the same day. Meals were ruled by "Mother" Oberin. When she sat, we sat. When she ate, we ate. When she stopped eating, we stopped.

Just as in previous schools I found overly strict instructors among our teaching staff. But for fear of losing my opportunity to study I tried my best to get favorable marks.

One day our chief surgeon asked me why I wanted to become a nurse. I replied that it was a suitable profession for a woman and that secretarial work did not appeal to me.

To my surprise he said, "To be a nurse is fine, Irene, but don't leave out finding a good husband. Do you really want to become a career nurse?"

I looked at him in utter disbelief. Seeing my astonishment he went on to say, "Look at those old *dragoners* (battle-axes). Take a closer look at our chief nurses. They have lost much of their femininity. They are like sergeants. They walk like sergeants, talk like sergeants, and order patients around. Don't become one of them."

After his remark I took a more critical look at the head nurses. Many of them really were as he described. Their war experiences made them what they were now. But others were strongly feminine, beautiful, vibrant women doing the work they loved to do. So I dismissed his comments and continued to enjoy my work as a nurse.

Once I worked in the dermatology ward where 42 beds were filled with patients from the uranium mines. Although they were warned of the danger, these men drank the contaminated underground water when they were thirsty. They developed an acne type rash that covered the entire body, even the face, causing intense itching. Doctors instructed us to brush a salve over the patient's entire body. They also gave patients an oral medication, however I doubted its effectiveness. I was often in charge of this ward after the evening meal, between the day and night shifts.

This ward adjoined a lounge in which many patients spent most of their daytime hours. They were allowed to walk around and were expected to make their own beds and keep their area tidy. One evening, while administering medication and counting heads to see that everyone was present, I discovered one patient was missing. If I left the ward to search for him no nurse would be left on the ward and this would be against regulations.

In order to make a search I ordered all patients into their rooms. Although they grumbled, I knew they would stay there. Quickly I started my search. Not finding the patient inside the immediate area, I went through a door marked "emergency" which exited into the park. Other people were there but my patient was not. I walked deeper into the park. It was getting dark. As I was about to turn around and leave I saw him. Dressed only in his pajamas, he was preparing to hang himself on a tree. Angrily I rushed toward him and grabbed the rope away from his neck. His apparent respect for me kept him from physically taking the rope back, although he was much larger than me. He fell to his knees and cried like a child.

"I cannot go on living with this itching all over my body. Nothing helps. I want to die!"

Taking him by the hand and talking calmly, I led him back into the building. I threw the rope into the greenhouse as we passed and took him to the treatment room and gave him an extra layer of salve on his body. I promised him I would not talk about this incident to anyone, since attempted suicide was punishable by law.

Days later when he said to others in front of me, "Sister Irene, you saved my life," I was very uncomfortable. Since I had not reported the incident, I was relieved when he recovered enough to be sent home.

The medical needs of men from the uranium mines increased and administrative changes were made to accommodate them. Rabenstein Hospital was taken over by Wismut A.G., an organization which was formed after the war by the Russian and German Governments. The purpose of Wismut was to remove ore from the Silver Mountains of the Erzgebirge and its first priority was the uranium.

Working in a hospital owned by Wismut provided us with extra food rations. We bought lavish amounts of food in a special Wismut store while other people were still very hungry.

I saved much of those food ration stamps and Ortwin came by to shop with me and carry the food home. Each time he arrived at the Hospital gate I was notified by the guards. Ortwin, age 17 and tall for his age, explained over and over that he was my brother and not my boyfriend. We secretly laughed about all the fuss and knew we were watched constantly by suspicious eyes when he came to visit.

At the end of my first year of training I was allowed a one month vacation. Wearing my uniform home seemed a bit awkward but people expected it that way. To my amazement, neighbors in the village of Euba came to me for help with minor accidents.

I was now 20 years old. Ortwin was 17; Hartmut 16; Claus, 10; and Christine, 5. Our home was full of merry sounds with much clowning and laughter. I loved to dance and Saturday night dances found me with many dancing partners.

"I never knew we had so many friends until you came home, Irene," Ortwin teased.

Karl-Heinz, my old friend from childhood days in Chemnitz, came to see me. We laughed about the game we called the "dating game" and cried about the loss of Esther and other dear friends. He joined in singing with all our friends as I played my accordion on Krista's porch.

Karl-Heinz came on my days off and we became close friends again. His fond attention brought smiles and knowing looks from friends as they watched us dance. Even Mama soon saw his romantic interest in me.

"He's a handsome young man, Irene," she said. "That dark wavy hair and those deep green eyes could capture any girl's heart. Are you going to finish your training or let marriage come into your life now?"

"Karl-Heinz has several years of training before he will be a qualified draftsman, Mama," I answered. "We've both decided to wait."

We had just finished clearing up the evening meal when Karl-Heinz walked into the room. He surprised me by saying, "I love Irene, Mutter Ella." He hesitated, watching both of us, then continued. "I want Irene to promise she will wait for me until I finish school and get a job."

"It's too soon to plan marriage," we both agreed.

"Things will work out for us," he said, putting his arm around my waist. "It just takes time."

Mama looked relieved by our statements. Taking both our hands in hers she said, "I'm sure you two will do the right thing. Do come see us often, Karl-Heinz."

I promised to wait for Karl-Heinz but neither of us could know the changing winds that would intervene the next year.

My family and I revisited Dresden during my vacation and were dismayed to see the demolished buildings and destroyed bridges. Here again I saw the rubble-women slowly cleaning and salvaging usable bricks. A monument should be built to these brave women. They deserve it much more than any politician.

We took a river boat to Pillnitz Castle. How small the castle seemed now. In my memory it had been much larger. Although the famous restaurant on the hill was closed, we rode the cable car to the top of the hill and sat outside looking down on Dresden, now crushed by war. This is where we said goodbye to Papa for the last time. Mama's sad expression and tears told how deep her grief was in this city where we had once enjoyed much family fun.

We went home feeling sad and empty. Our trip on the train was so different from our happy but bumpy rides in Papa's *dreirad* (three-wheel bike).

HOME

Mama's application to move back into Chemnitz was postponed since she was unable to help with cleaning up rubble. Christine and Claus were too young to leave unattended and this work was a required condition if she moved into the city. As I started my second year of training in the summer of 1950, we heard rumors that the Russians wanted to take over Rabenstein Hospital. At first we only saw a few Russians: women doctors, and some soldiers and officers who performed the duties of occupation.

Just as I began to worry about our school for nursing being closed, the news came. It was all settled. Half of us were to be transferred to Annaberg, the other half to Wiesen. We had no choice about our transfer and if we wanted to earn our degrees we would have to go where they sent us. Even doctors were being transferred. We packed our personal things and climbed into waiting trucks. The canvas sides were rolled down. So our view was blocked but the rain was kept out as we were driven to the town of Wiesen. I had never heard of Wiesen or Wiesenburg, two small towns a good 25 miles distance from Zwickau. Many of those medieval picturesque small towns had no railstop and people walked many miles to Wiesenburg to catch a train into Zwickau. Our hospital, once a home for the elderly, was now renovated to serve patients from the uranium mines. However, there was no school in our new hospital in Wiesen, so we traveled to nearby Schneeberg to finish our nurses' training. Even though our new school of nursing was not as strict as Rabenstein, we still received instruction in Communism along with our classes in nursing. The Communist regime was trying to get a good grip on our people and they were not going to let us be indifferent about it.

Nurses were not housed in the Wiesen Hospital. One of the lucky few, I lived in a two-room apartment above a general store across the street from the Wiesenburg rail road station. I shared this with a student nurse, Gretl. She had come as a refugee from Silesia and somehow got stuck in East Germany.

About twenty years my senior, Gretl had a good sense of humor and enjoyed an excellent professional standing among her fellow nurses. Due to our age difference I came to regard Gretl as an adviser and a little like an older sister. She had clear skin, short brown hair and brown eyes. Her legs were attractive enough that men teased her in a flattering way, and she was very witty to let them know it was all a joke. A boyfriend she had at the time was more like an escort, an actor turned uranium mine worker because of the better pay and food rations. But once an actor, always an actor, and we had great fun when he performed his past roles only for us.

Our landlady, Old Buschin as we called her, was in her late 70's. She wore a wig and we always wondered where she got it from. False teeth were much harder to get so she did not have any. Once wealthy, she lost everything to the new government. She formerly owned an entire building complex and several stores in it. We lived in one of the buildings where she lived. Two sons she lost in the war and her husband died during the conflict in an accident. Now she was alone.

When the state took possession of her store and buildings, she was allowed to live rent-free in only two rooms of her four-room apartment. Gretl and I rented the other two plainly furnished rooms. The door between our apartments was locked and a couch placed in front of it. The water faucet was outside in the hallway and we shared the bathroom. Frau Buschin's income consisted of our rent plus a few Mark's from her social security. She was resourceful though, she remodeled her upstairs storage room in the attic into living quarters for a middle-age miner called Bruno.

During evening hours we could hear Bruno singing to our landlady and we heard her laughing. It was a good thing for them to spend their evenings together, since life was very dull in those days.

We were given more responsibilities in the hospital as we were expected to be RNs soon anyway since we already had the same duties. I took care of anything that came up in the ward where I worked. I made rounds with the doctors and was very conscientious about my assignments and soon earned compliments from patients. Many patients said that "I had a light hand" when giving shots. In those days, instruments of all kinds had to be sterilized by us as there was no such thing as "throw away supplies."

Doctor I____. said to me "People with blood type B are daredevils, Irene. They'll try things even when they're not sure they can do it. You know, you and I have blood type B."

I laughed at this remark. However, I soon became the right hand to the head nurse in the women's ward, even though I was considered much too young for the job. The women's ward contained female patients who had surgery, gynecological problems, or job-related

16

accidents. On surgery days I was often assigned to help doctors in the operating room. I went more often than duty required, because I wanted to learn as much as I could.

Every second week the police hauled a dozen or so prostitutes into our hospital for examinations. We checked them for gonorrhea and took blood samples for syphilis. Usually four out of twelve were diseased. Those without any sign of disease were taken to a work camp. Those with a disease went into a jail hospital for treatment and then to a work camp.

One day, Doctor Z_____ had to decide to perform an abortion on a pregnant prostitute with syphilis. If she had given birth to this baby, the possibility existed that the child would be born blind. False labor was induced. The girl cried and we worked, pushed and sweated with her for hours until the fetus finally came out.

This must have been an old fashioned procedure, but the girl was too far along to do it any other way. The fetus was a completely formed baby boy. I felt so sad. I turned my head and cried for this lost life.

Our political teachers called venereal diseases the *capitalistic diseases*. Everything they disliked was labeled "capitalistic." On the other hand, all technical achievements were invented by the Russians. We secretly laughed about those foolish claims.

The order came that we must meet once each week to learn how to become better Communists. One-fifth of the hospital personnel now wore party pins. They reminded me of the Nazi pins our school teachers wore. Once seated in a meeting, a list was sent around with instructions to "sign your name." Party authorities checked those who came to the meetings and reprimanded those who did not attend.

Since the village blackboard bulletin at the corner of the hospital grounds was our only link with the world beyond our community, I told Gretl I would love to buy a radio. One day we went to find one and tried many shops in different cities. We were so exhausted, but used all our free time for many weeks until we spotted one. Small and simple, it made sounds and it worked! We bought it, and we took it home with us where it provided news and some music to lighten our study hours. Every Tuesday night I remember we tried to stay home to listen to classical music, and some people who had no radio came to join us.

In the usual way, we began to hear about the "advantages" people would have if the government took over all the farms in East Germany, which they already had in some places. Farmers would become workers on their own farms and receive a salary, but had no more say as to what would be planted. Such decisions were not their concern anymore.

People who owned nice houses were allowed to still live in the homes. If however they wanted to move for any reason, they would lose the house. They were not allowed to sell their house, neither could they will it to their children since it now belonged to the State. Also factories and businesses of all kinds were taken over by the State. Already in effect in 1946 this law called "Volksentscheid" (resolution of the people) expropriated anything that was of value. By 1949 there were not many if any private businesses left. All this was done for the "protection" of the people. People who owned no real estate were told to sign petitions that "the people" demanded that all farms and properties become part of the state and collective farm called "Kolchose."

Near Wiesen was a beautiful little town named Kirschberg. One could feel that this place had lots of history with its medieval buildings, although now it consisted mostly of farmland. I watched this beautiful village being turned into a collective farm, Co-op. All fields became government property and no farmer was allowed to make any decision regarding the land. The farmer would also be punished with jail time should he butcher one of his own chickens or pigs since they no longer belonged to him either. This is how the tentacles of the Communist State encircled village after village and farm after farm into large collectives.

Farmers, as well as the owners of other large enterprises and private businesses, were told that under Communism they would be paid a salary for their work. Savings were no longer needed since the State would provide for them now and when they became old. Pensions would be calculated according to each person's job. There would be a file on every person. All health care and education for children would be provided by the State and the State would select the kind of educational training to be given. "Good workers" and people who were "cooperative" would receive a paid vacation at a popular resort once a year. If they were not productive workers, they should not expect lavish vacations. "The State is generous with the people" was often the subject in our classes on Communism. Many people, myself included, deeply resented the way our lives had become. We felt we were becoming as oppressed under Russian occupation as we had been under Nazis control.

Among our political watchdogs, titled "culture directors," and assigned by the Communist Party, was Rudolf, a little man with feet so quiet he could come up behind you and never make a sound. He delivered many boring lectures on Communism.

On the southern side the hospital had large balconies where we aired beds. One unfortunate day, I sat on one of these balconies with a few nurses and Rudolf. During conversations he always tried to deliver his doctrine to us. I leaned over toward Rudolf and said, "Come on, Rudolf, you yourself can't believe all this nonsense." I leaned closer and said, "Do you really believe what you teach us?"

Two nurses gasped. Rudolf looked me straight in the eye, bit his lower lip and said nothing. I straightened up, still looking at Rudolf and waiting for an answer, but none came. Living with lies day after day, year after year, makes a person physically ill. I always had this nasty feeling about lying. I wanted to shout out what I felt but I knew I should not. I'll never know what made me say it but now that I had I knew I had to live with the consequences.

I suspected that Rudolf's job was to spy and look for people with ideas like mine. He left and did not answer me, but I was warned by my coworkers that he would make me pay for my careless words. After duty hours, I was ordered to come to Rudolf's office. He preached to me about how young I was and that he did not want to ruin my life. If I would say that I was sorry, he might be able to "save" me.

I was ordered to spend my evenings "constructively" by learning how to play chess. Under normal circumstances, people, myself included, would have liked chess. But it was also a favorite Russian game and therefore hated. Nevertheless, it was a mild punishment and I was now forced to spend many evenings after work learning and playing chess. Rudolf's office became a chess tournament room and all individuals with dissident thoughts were regularly assembled. Among those gathered, there were a few nurses and over eighty percent of our doctors. Conversation was not allowed, only the study of chess. Even so, our free evenings were lost.

***

My first vacation provided by the State was not to a place where I really wanted to go, but I had to go where I was told. I was sent to Gral Mueritz, a beach resort on the northern shore of East Germany. The more desirable place, the Island of Ruegen, was not available to me.

In spite of the warnings that Gral Mueritz would be a dull place, I wanted to get away and was looking forward to getting a good rest. By going to Gral Mueritz, I could stay six weeks. If I had gone home my leave would have been only twenty-one days. I wanted to see the ocean and this was my only chance.

My new vacation clothes, which were hard to come by, consisted of a bathrobe suitable for beach wear and a two piece beige dress trimmed with brown that felt suspiciously like paper. The sales girl acted as if she had done me a big favor by selling it to me. Since I felt desperate for some new clothes and since the dress did look nice on me, I bought it.

Transportation to Gral Mueritz was on a special train provided just for vacationers. We sat on clean but hard wooden benches, definitely not comfortable. The cars were crowded but there was a seat for everyone. After many hours, when the benches became unbearable, we stood for short periods of time. No food or drink was served. But being excited about going on a vacation, we overlooked our hunger and the other inconveniences. We talked for a while, then, feeling very tired, we closed our eyes. Sleep was difficult as the lights on the train were very glaring and the speakers constantly blared loud music into our ears. Overtired children behaved well enough and parents, happy to get a vacation spot to Gral Mueritz, kept a sharp eye on them.

Our trip should not have taken more than six hours but instead it took us one entire day and one entire night. We knew that many times the whole train was delayed on dead railroad tracks to let more important trains pass. At the end of our journey, with our luggage in hand, we stood in line for lodging in hotels or boarding houses, now all owned by the State. In a vacation house I was assigned to a room with four beds in it. After I plunked down on one of the beds two more girls that I did not know arrived. The three of us would spend the next six weeks together. The rules of the house were that we had to care for our own room ourselves. All the occupants on our floor of six bedrooms shared only one bathroom. We would be allowed to go into the village hotels only when there was entertainment or to use the reading rooms.

I unpacked quickly and rushed to get to the bathroom. After a trip like we had just endured, everyone wanted to take a shower before anything else. There was a long line outside the bathroom door.

I wanted to see the Baltic Sea as soon as possible, so I left the house and ran down to the dunes. I climbed the sandy slopes, which were pegged with pines where buckets were attached to the older trees to draw pungent pine oil for medical and chemical uses.

I could hear the pounding waves. Up one more dune and there it was, rolling forever against Germany's shore--a cold blue-grey sea rippling into surging froth. The white sand lay serene and quiet as this giant of a sea roared toward me and then retreated, spending its energy in eternal motion.

The air was invigorating and rushed through my hair as I ran down the dunes and into the water where cold water flushed around my ankles.

"This is life! This is freedom!"

Nearby I could see the wicker beach baskets. They were six feet high, and inside there was a two seat bench. One could lift up the seat and stuff valuables inside, then lock it up with a padlock to keep things safe when going swimming or on a boat ride. I have nowhere else seen such convenient wicker beach baskets except in Germany. They look like huge hampers, but they serve as combination dressing rooms and shelters in rainy weather for bathers. Judging by the number of vacationers and the available beach baskets, one would have to get up very early to rent one. Each beach basket appeared to be occupied.

Shallow wooden boats were being rowed out from the shoreline. No motors could be heard, just the rush of the sea as it broke on the white sandy shore. Farther out, what looked like a ship's mast stuck out of the water at a crazy angle. No doubt a sunken ship from previous years and now of no apparent interest to anyone.

"There are no sharks to fear," a vacationer said. "The water is too cold. The herring and eel are abundant though."

After breathing deeply of the fresh air, I walked back to my boarding house. There I learned we would be eating all our meals in a dining room located in the largest hotel in the village. We were to have a specific table and strict meal schedules. Our breakfast, the last of three settings, would be from 8:30 to 9:00 a.m.

Our food was the same as what I ate at home, except eel was served more frequently. Ever since I knew that eel feed on dead humans, I did not care much for it. But in a time when food was rationed, I ate it, and it was provided in sufficient amounts. Everyone ate from the same menu, no choices were permitted. There were no sandwiches to take out and no other food available. Those going on all-day trips went without meals. I am sure that when people did not show up at meal time, it was reported.

My roommates, Lone and Linda, were pleasant and we shared some of our activities. We went to a dance one evening where we danced a few times then just sat around. The men seemed dull. An invitation to play soccer on the beach with some boys was fun until our shins got banged up and we quit. We certainly didn't know soccer was such a mean sport. Another day we were able to rent a beach basket and we talked and laughed, built sand castles, then went swimming in the still cold water.

The important thing for me was the sea. Once I walked along the beach a whole day, forgetting both lunch and dinner. I walked where there were no people--just myself and the sea. It seemed so free and it wreathed in rhythmic swells and continually roared a song of freedom. I sang back to it as I walked along its shore.

Die Gedanken sind frei, wer kann sie erraten?
Sie fliehen vorbei, wie naechtliche Schatten.
Kein Mensch kann sie wissen, kein Jaeger sie schiessen,
Es bleibet dabei: Die Gedanken sind frei!

Ich denk' was ich mag und was mich begluecket,
doch alles in der still', und wie es sich schicket.
Mein Wunsch und begehren karin niemand verwehren
Es bleibet dabei, die Gedanken sind frei
(Part of an old German folk song)

English translation:
My thoughts they are free, no one can ever guess them.
They flee away, like shadows in the night.
No human can know, no hunter can shoot,
I declare to the sea, my thoughts they are free!

I think what I like, and what makes me happy,
be still my soul, and do what you are told!

25

but my wish, my desire, no one can take away,

I declare to the sea, my thoughts they are free!

Out of nowhere stepped an armed guard. Suddenly I was back in the real world of an armed police State.

"Where are you going, Fraulein? Turn around! Turn around! What are you doing out here? Waiting for a boat that will take you to Denmark, eh?"

"Don't get excited, I am going." *Everything is guarded*, I thought. Always big brother was watching us. It was so depressing. I looked back the way I had come. There was no village in sight, I must have walked several miles. I turned around and started back. A little frightened, I lengthened my stride to put distance between myself and the guard.

As I returned to my room I thought about leaving East Germany. The song "Nun Adieu Du Mein Lieb' Heimatland" kept running through my mind. The wind and the sea caught my song and carried it to somewhere in the future.

"Nun adieu, du mein lieb Heimatland,

Lieb Heimatland adieu!

Es geht jetzt fort zum fremden Strand,

Lieb Heimatland, adieu!

Und so sing ich denn mit frohem Mut

, wie man singet, wenn man wandern tut,

Lieb Heimatland adieu!

Wie du lachst mit deines Himmels blau,

Lieb Heimatland adieu!

Wie du gruessest mich mit Feld und Au,

Lieb Heimatland adieu!

Gott weiss, zu dir steht stets mein Sinn;

Nur etzt zur Ferne muss ich hin,

Lieb Heimatland adieu!

"Begleitest mich, du lieber Fluss,

Lieb Heirnatland adieu!

es ist traurig das ich fort hier muss,

Lieb Heirnatland adieu!

Von moos'gen Stein am wald'gen Tal,

Da gruess ich dich zum letzten Mal,

Lieb Heimatland, adieu!

(Old German folksong)

English translation:

Now, farewell oh you my Native Land,

You my Native Land, farewell.

I am on my way to foreign lands,

You my Native land, goodbye,

And so I shall sing a cheerful song,

as one sings when one is moving on

You, my Native Land, goodbye!

Oh, how blue your sky does smile at me

You my Native Land goodbye!

Fields and meadows are saluting me,

You my Native Land goodbye!

God knows, I loved you all my life,

but away it pulls me with much might.

You my Native land, goodbye!

You dear river you accompany me,

You my Native Land goodbye

Are you mourning that I'm leaving thee,

You my Native Land, goodbye!

From the green downstream and stony height,

I salute you now this final time,

You my Native Land, goodbye.

One cool day I took my letter writing materials, found a large table in the lounge of one of the big hotels and wrote to Mama, Karl-Heinz and a few friends.

Suddenly a voice over the loudspeaker filled the air. "All persons not employed by Wismut A.G. must leave the resort." We learned that some vacationers had secretly rented some boats in the hope of getting to Denmark. Silently I prayed that those people with children in their boat would reach the safe shores of Denmark and freedom. Many people became angry, saying they all had to suffer because a few had defected. In the confusion, wives and children were being sent home without their husbands. This caused more anger and couples began leaving early, creating vacancies the State had not counted on. Some vacationers were crying from the sheer frustration of it all.

In disgust I left and walked around the resort, now rapidly emptying of vacationers. I walked into the fishing village of Gral, stopping at a gift shop where I bought two rings set with amber, a cigarette holder and a pendant all made out of amber. Amber was big business there. Amber is harvested from the sea, and it is said that once upon a time Germany and the Baltic countries were joined. Only after the Big Flood, they parted and became separate. All the pine forests sank into the Baltic Sea. During the following centuries, the pine trees still bleeding under the water, their sap turned into beautiful amber. A piece of amber with an insect caught in it was exceptionally precious.

When I returned to my quarters I washed my new dress. It turned out to be paper--more disappointment. I had paid half a month's salary for this paper dress.

With two more weeks of vacation left, my roommates and I found little to interest us in Gral Mueritz. We requested permission to leave, but were told that was out of the question. If we left early our vacation would be cut short and we would have to go back to work immediately. If we stayed, we could enjoy two more weeks of the sea, but things were not the same anymore. We got permission to visit a nearby city, Rostock, although we had to promise to sign-in in the evening. Rostock must once have been a very interesting city. Now, however, in the harbor we saw a Russian ship and it sure looked different than the ones I had seen in the Western countries. It was a freighter that had to load up merchandise. Everybody was shouting in

Russian. We stopped and watched, thinking that this ship might go to Siberia where all the labor camps were. I always got goose bumps thinking about labor camps.

Hungry and cold, we returned from our outing only to find that in Gral Mueritz the dining room was closed. In Rostock, the few things they had were on ration cards. So that day was without provision. Of course, that made the day not what it should have been.

We plotted how we could get away from it all. With two more weeks vacation left, we wanted to go to Berlin. Only when we promised we would go straight home, was permission given to leave the resort. When we arrived in Berlin we decided to stay in the city. Linda's aunt lived in West Berlin. This knowledge, along with my past adventures in crossing borders, aroused a sense of adventure in me that I could not resist.

We cleaned up in the washroom of the railroad station, checked our suitcases into lockers and found our way to the Brandenburger Gate. The wall was not built yet. East German police with rifles and Russian guards carrying the usual machine guns strapped over their shoulders were walking around watching everyone.

Being very careful to appear nonchalant, we slowly inched our way closer to the big gate. We could see the West German police on the other side.

"Now!" I whispered.

I led and Lorie and Linda followed. We walked boldly toward the gate. Although we could feel eyes on our backs, people were staring at us, no one shouted and no one shot for a long scary minute. We must have caught them by surprise. Their propaganda loudspeakers were going 24 hours a day, telling people to stay in the workers' paradise. Nobody had the courage to just do what we were doing, since everyone was sure the guards would fire. We kept walking, not daring to turn around.

The West German police looked toward us and gestured in a friendly manner to keep going. This was all the encouragement we needed. If we felt uncertain we did not show it. Suddenly we heard shouting and turned to see the East German police shouting at each other and Russian patrols gesturing and waving their weapons about. It was a very angry scene. It must have been about us. The West German police laughed and welcomed us.

Following a policeman's directions, we walked to Charlottenburg where we were welcomed by Linda's aunt and two teenage cousins, Fritz and Kurt.

For several days we enjoyed the freedom of West Berlin. We walked up and down the famous "Kurfuerstendamm," which they called "Ku-Damm," where we feasted our eyes on the colorful merchandise displayed in the shop windows. The drab grays that dominated East Germany were in sharp contrast to this lively scene of action and color.

I was not prepared for the loss I took when I exchanged five East Marks for only one West Mark. That made it seem like I worked for only a fifth of my monthly salary, which was then about 400 East Marks. I learned that for the same job in the West I could make a little more than 450 West Marks a month, which for 1950 was a very good salary, even in West Germany. I exchanged only enough East Marks to buy some post cards and a ticket to a movie.

We later sat in an outdoor coffeehouse and watched people walk by. We learned about travel between East and West. Although hundreds of police guarded the border, Fritz and Kurt found ways to slip by the armed guards on little side streets to attend Saturday dances in East Berlin. Beer was of course cheaper in East Berlin. Linda's aunt said she got her hair fixed only in East Berlin because it cost a fraction of what she would have to pay in West Berlin. I thought about how they came from the West to take advantage of the services in the East and paid very little. Then, with their Western passes, riding the Metro, which they affectionately called the U-Bahn (metro train), they could go back and forth without fear. It was not fair.

Kurt and Fritz said the music and entertainment in East Berlin was alright and the drinks were much cheaper. I felt like everyone wanted the most out of their money. Still, the tightened security of the wall was yet to come.

Friends of Linda's aunt gave us second-hand dresses, nylons and shoes. The bitter experience of washing my paper dress into a pulp seemed less dreadful.

As my vacation came to an end I realized I wanted the freedom of West Germany. The West was then accepting East Germans as refugees, something they could not do when I crossed the border a few years ago near Sonneberg. It seemed to me that it would be easier to get into the West through Berlin. However, I did not want to jeopardize my training just now. A graduate nurse would find it easier in West Germany when seeking employment.

We boarded the U-Bahn, traveled back into East Berlin, picked up our suitcases and caught the train to Leipzig. We traveled on to Zwickau where Lone and Linda lived, and afterwards I caught a train home to Wiesenburg.

BACK TO WORK

When I returned to work I found more people had joined the Communist Party to put themselves in better employment situations. Even Herr Viehstig, a custodian who only had an elementary education at the time, was advanced to be our second Culture Director. He used to go around bringing small bottles of champagne to those who were very seriously ill and were most likely to die. When he left the room he said, "To have a happy ascension." Some people actually laughed and took it as a joke. This unfortunate gesture was very sad for those receiving the gift, though they often wanted more of the bubbling stuff.

It was important to be respectful toward Culture Directors, and now we had two of them. They had the power to send people away for severe punishment and they did. Sister Wally, an RN, and her husband were arrested after her husband was accused of having done some work for the West. Authorities felt Sister Wally must have known about his activities, so she was also arrested. She was a real loss to our nursing staff. We never heard how many years people were sentenced to serve, and I never saw her again.

How strange life can be. When Sister Wally was arrested some people spoke in whispers about what had happened. They tried to look the other way. Sadly, some of those same people got arrested only a few years later. The heavy hand of communism snatched people from our midst just as the Nazis had taken our Jewish neighbors. This had a very sobering effect upon all of us.

Since our hospital existed solely to care for people working in the uranium mines, most of our patients suffered from accidents caused by explosions, falls, or injuries caused when work was pushed at high speed. In spite of these hazards, jobs in the uranium mines remained desirable for several reasons. Following the war, starvation was so great that many people were seeking employment with the Wismut. Since the Wismut was the only place to get more food, many educated men worked right alongside the uneducated. The Wismut provided protective outer clothing to all who signed contracts to work and from then on, everyone looked the same. Workers were paid according to how much and how fast they dug the pitch-blend and ore.

People died from accidents in the mines and our hospital beds were filled to capacity. During the years I worked there, another much larger hospital was built in Erlabrunn closer to the mining area. The wages were good, but most importantly all food rations were better there than in any other place in East Germany.

Doctors worked with insufficient medical supplies. Therefore, many people could not be saved. This frustrated our doctors over the years. I know many of them made it to West Germany.

During the Christmas season in 1950, I played my accordion during some of my off-duty hours to entertain the patients. On Christmas Day a group of male patients, dressed in grey house robes, sat like figures of stone in the lounge. Seeing their despondency, I played my accordion while a few of them sang the old Christmas songs.

35

Their eyes saw far beyond the room we were in. I knew they were thinking of their families. Some started sobbing loudly and I was sad that I could not comfort them. Plates were passed but all we had to put on them was an apple. These men did not usually reveal their inner feelings but that forlorn apple did it.

Quickly I broke up the Christmas gathering, knowing that it had not been such a good idea. I should not have reminded them of Christmas at all. No clergyman ever visited our hospital but religious services were needed by all of us. I felt anger toward our Culture Directors. Where were they? Couldn't they do more than the useless work for the Communist Party?

Giving permission to leave the lights on longer for reading, I went to my duty room. The entire hospital seemed unusually quiet. Someone knocked softly on the door. I opened it to see a patient standing in the half-darkened hall.

"Yes? What is it?" I asked.

"We thought, well, we just thought--we don't have much to give you. But we made this for you."

I opened the door wider. Two more patients stood there, holding out a small package. I took the package from their outstretched hands but before I could say anything, they turned and hurriedly walked back toward their rooms.

"Thank you and Merry Christmas," I said to a hallway that was empty and quiet again.

I opened the packages to find two wooden carvings, an Erzgebirge angel and an ore miner, made into a candle holder. How beautiful they were. Immediately, they became my most treasured gifts. I thought of my family and how I missed them.

Many patients cried quietly as they went to sleep that Christmas.

During the month of January we started the nursing examinations that would lead to diplomas in April. We learned that further study was available for those wanting to become doctor's assistants. I would have welcomed more studies, but not under those conditions. For the present, being a nurse was enough and very rewarding.

Time flew by, then came the finals. The advice was the same as when I first applied to study nursing, "Speak little and be precise when answering medical questions, but talk at great length when asked political questions."

Finals took three days. Each day, in fresh clean uniforms, we appeared before the examining board to chalk up our points. I experienced a feeling of real achievement when I learned I had passed the State examinations. A small but important freedom we enjoyed as registered nurses was to push our caps back and show more hair. But the cap was starched so stiff that it had already cut off lots of my hair on both sides of my head.

I got vacation leave and went home just in time to help Mama move into Chemnitz. Her apartment was in the same building where Grandma Thekla had lived. People were still cleaning bricks to salvage material to build again some day, although I never saw men doing this backbreaking work. Too many men were killed in the war, and many others had run to the West.

Uncle Albert and Aunt Martha wanted to open a butchery again but they would have to build one from the rubble. This would mean thousands of hours of work before they could open for business. No loans were available to buy new materials. If there would be another butchery, it would most likely belong to the state.

Things seemed so dreary for people trying to earn a livelihood in our destroyed city.

I returned to Wiesen to work on the Surgery and Gynecology wards. Gretl and I continued to share our two-room apartment.

During my off duty hours I continued playing my accordion for patients. Eventually our little radio had stopped playing, and no one could fix it. There were no other radios, no movies, and I never saw a magazine of any kind. There was no entertainment other than propaganda loudspeakers piping some music into the hospital rooms, though it was frequently interrupted with lots of praise for the Soviet Army and talk about the Party.

When the Cultural Directors saw how much patients liked to sing along with me, they promised to arrange for touring groups of entertainers to come to the hospital. Although infrequent, this recreation was welcomed by everyone.

Returning home one evening, we found a large bouquet of flowers in front of our door. No card was enclosed. Since Gretl knew nothing about it, I supposed they were from the patients I had played songs for and thought little more about it. The next day another bouquet awaited our return from work and still no note accompanied the flowers.

Each day for the next two weeks a bouquet arrived. Our two-room apartment began to resemble a flower shop. Since there were no florists in our area and the flowers were the same colors as some blooming in the hospital gardens, our curiosity grew with each bouquet. I asked the hospital gardener about the flowers. He denied knowing about them. I asked the gardener's assistant, who seemed to know something but was reluctant to talk. After bribing him with cigarettes, he told me they were from a patient on the third floor. This was a surprise since neither Gretl nor I worked on this floor.

Seeking the anonymous giver, I walked up to the third floor. On the way I met Doctor W_____, a woman medical intern, whose well known abruptness left her with few close friends among our staff.

"What are you doing up here?" she demanded.

While I was trying to answer her, I noticed a patient behind her began motioning for me to leave indicating that he would contact me later. Confused, and a little surprised, I mumbled something and left.

I entered the nurses' room where patients were not allowed in except by permission. Soon I answered a knock at the door from the male patient I had seen upstairs. I invited him in.

"I did not send you the flowers," he started. "A friend of mine is sending them to you. He is in love with you, and he isn't sure if you will talk to him."

My astonishment left me speechless. He went on to say, "He is a schoolteacher but he works as an *Obersteiger* for the Wismut in Schneeberg."

"I have always made it clear to patients that I will tolerate no nonsense." I knew male patients often became infatuated with nurses, especially when they started to recover. I had seen these flirtations and wanted no association with them. This situation was ridiculous,

39

since I didn't even know the man he was talking about. My visitor was waiting for an answer.

"He must stop sending me flowers. I will tell him so myself." My visitor left, looking downhearted.

During visiting hours I returned to the third floor room. There were at least five people, all patients, in a room with only two beds. Everyone seemed excited and expectant of my arrival. I was certainly not known to make friendly visits to patients during visiting hours.

Visiting hours were strictly observed and once they were over, visitors who often came from far away, had to depart the hospital grounds. A guard at the grounds' gate saw to it that people would leave.

As I had entered the room, I asked, "Where is the man who sent me flowers?" Everyone motioned to one bed. I turned and looked into the bluest eyes and the reddest boyish face I've ever seen. His flushed face showed embarrassment but his eyes begged me to understand. I had not expected him to be so darn good looking. My resolve began to weaken.

Someone shoved a chair at me and I sat down still looking at those sparkling blue eyes. He could not have been more than five or six years older than I was.

"I don't want you to send me any more flowers," I began as Doctor W_____ came into the room. Doctor W_____ stared at me in disbelief, then turned and ran down the corridor. Puzzled by her behavior and thinking she would report me, I followed her. At the top of the stairs a patient caught up with me, saying, "You must talk to him."

"Not now and not here. Later!" I ran to the duty room. There sat Doctor W_____ crying. She looked up and said, "He is mine!" Then she burst into tears again.

How complicated things had become. I didn't even know the patient's name. Also, why was Doctor W_____ interested in this man when everyone knew the rule never to have an affair with a patient. What was so special about this one?

Doctor W_____ must care for him very much to be so upset, I thought. She probably knew about the flowers? I felt helpless, a little flattered and angry.

"How could you let yourself go on like this for a younger man and a patient at that?" I asked and left, not waiting for her answer.

How ridiculous, I thought. I was now involved in a triangle and it was all his fault. Why did he have to be so handsome? I couldn't forget those blue eyes and his flushed boyish face. I smiled and went on about my work.

As I walked out of the building to go home that evening, the third floor patient, dressed in a robe, was waiting for me beside the door.

As I approached him he said, "I'm sorry if I caused you any problem, but I do want to talk to you."

"Start first by telling me your name."

"Sister Irene, I am Volker Hofmann."

"Yes. Do you have permission to be up and about? What are you in for?"

"Pneumonia. I'm going to be released next week. May I see you?" His face was flushing red again.

Having pneumonia was a four week stay in the hospital in those days. Other illnesses also took much longer to treat than in our day.

"You know nurses cannot mix socially with patients. Walk down that hall and I'll talk to you in a few minutes." I walked away from him, then turned and followed him as he walked toward the hall I had indicated. He was tall, with broad shoulders, muscular, but not thin.

"You sent me flowers?" I asked, looking up into his very blue eyes. "Why me? How did you find out about me?"

"I've heard you play your accordion out on the balcony. I like your music and singing and you have helped everyone to feel better. Even the doctors and nurses join in the singing. I wanted to be your friend."

"I'm not sure, you know it is forbidden that nurses and--"

"I know," he interrupted. "Perhaps I can get a pass from the doctor on your free day and we--"

"Are you able to go out of the hospital now?" I was stalling for time. I shouldn't see him but I did want to know more about him. "Thursday is my free day but where?"

"If I can get a pass, let's meet at the train station. Just one day, please?" His smile was disarming.

I agreed. I don't know how but he got a pass to leave the hospital for a whole day. We boarded the train and went to Zwickau. He wore a blue suit which looked a lot like the old Air Force uniform, a leftover from the war. He, just like everyone else, could not get civilian clothes. People were still in World War II uniforms, only without the markings. Even so, he made a handsome figure. Most people wore ill fitting clothes because that was all there was.

I liked his manners, so gentleman like. It would flatter any woman to be with a man so courteous.

We sat at a table by a large window upstairs in the Ring Kaffee and started to get acquainted.

"During the last year of the war I worked in an office in Berlin. Until I was called into the Air Force I studied at the University of Berlin. Mother and Father lived in Breslau and we became refugees in 1944-1945. They traveled west in a covered wagon and in that cold winter mother died of pneumonia."

"Do you have some Polish blood?" I asked.

"Yes, some."

"So do I. My father is from Galicia."

I began to feel more at ease with this pleasant young man whose blue eyes seemed so eager. We talked all day, telling each other about our families and our experiences during the war. After his mother's death, his father came to Berlin. Now they lived in Schneeberg. His father taught while Volker helped out directing plays at one of the schools there. Volker took a job in the Wismut in order to survive, like everyone else. In the evening, as a band started to play, we danced. His arms trembled when he held me. We circled the floor to many dance rhythms, laughing and feeling the closeness of one another. We drank *Danziger Goldwasser*, a popular liquor, and danced some more. Later, we went downstairs for dinner. The waiter asked for ration stamps first, money was secondary.

Our day was coming to an end. We liked each other and we both knew it. We caught the last train back to Wiesenburg, not sure when we could have another day together.

43

Gretl was still up reading so I poured myself a cup of chicory.

"Aha, you know you have stolen Doctor W_____'s man. She is going to get you for this," she teased. We laughed.

"Things have become complicated. You know I didn't know who sent all these flowers. What can I do?" I shrugged, smiling. Gretl had put all the flowers out in the hall for the night since the heavy fragrance would bother us sleeping. I went to sleep thinking about Volker's blue eyes.

After Volker was released from the hospital we spent most of our free hours together. It wasn't always easy to make our free days coincide especially when everyone became aware that we were dating. When my supervisor learned that I wanted to keep an appointment to see Volker, the request was often dismissed with "the schedule was already set, cannot make any changes..." I often wondered if Doctor W_____ had influenced my supervisor's decision.

When we were together, Volker often said it was "as if some splendid release from the world swept over us." For a few hours we forgot the difficult problems all around us, the constant propaganda about the Russia-German friendship, the Communist Five Year Plan, the Two Year Plan, and so on, and so on.

Most of our free hours were spent in the one and only restaurant in Oberschlema. We sat at a table by the window. We touched wine glasses, exchanged fond glances, and held hands. We danced when there was a band. Volker's strong arms encircled me with gentleness and warmth. He led me through dances we never wanted to end.

I knew Volker's attention to me was serious and that at some time in the future he would propose marriage. I knew too that to find a place to live together would be difficult. There was no furniture for sale in stores; there were no stores either. To start a home would mean that we would have to find some second hand stuff. Babies that, to continue my nursing career, would have to be raised in the *Kinderhort*. A *Kinderhort* was a State-run childcare center in which children learn from a very early age about Communism and the heroic Red Army. They were also told how bad we Germans were. I didn't want to face that yet. I wasn't ready to give up my independence--and yet I was more than fond of him.

I liked Volker for more than his charm and flattering compliments. There was a certain detachment born of self-control about Volker that distinguished him from other men. He seemed to have a patina of authority that had nothing to do with his position as an Obersteiger for the Wismut. It was somehow related solely to his own self esteem and outlook. This was evident at all times when I was with him: the way he introduced me to his friends, how he ordered our table in the restaurant and even in his conversation with my friends.

I sensed he would never allow himself to become irresponsibly drunk as we were both aware that many men were drinking heavily to deaden the frustrations of the times. Probably these frustrations accounted for Volker's serious nature. The little lines around his eyes and his mouth told me that the war had taken its toll.

When we walked arm in arm in the streets of Zwickau, he must have been pleasantly aware of the glances he received from other women. Secretly I hoped he was not aware of those flirtatious looks. He directed his attention toward me. I thought he was entirely without vanity concerning his good looks.

It was then that I started to fall in love with him. I took great pleasure in his comment that "I was his oasis." The first and last words he always said to me while we dated were, "Remember, I love you."

During warm summer months we walked along the Mulde River. When time permitted we even carried a picnic basket. Volker called me "Reneilienien" and I was thrilled to hear this endearing name.

One evening in August we were sitting on the bank of the Mulde River and there was a growing chorus of frogs in the warm summer air as the stars were beginning to twinkle. Volker took me in his arms and told me again of his love for me.

"Your loveliness had been evident from the first moment I saw you on the balcony playing your accordion. Even then I knew I wanted to be with you." He paused, then put his hand on my shoulder and turned me to look squarely at him.

"I love you, Reneilein. Will you marry me?"

"I've had a feeling for some time that this was coming. I just didn't expect it so soon. We haven't known each other very long. Are you sure?" I asked.

In the twilight the flecks of blue in his eyes were brilliant. I felt helpless when I looked into them.

"I didn't plan to ask you this evening, but now I'm glad I did." He paused because of my silence. "Will you, Renilein? Life will not be easy, it will be very difficult. But I suppose we have to make a new beginning sometime."

His face was close, his eyes so adoring. Suddenly I knew I wanted all the good things life could bring with Volker.

"Yes. Yes, dear Volker. I do love you."

His kiss was tender and possessive and I responded to his loving embrace.

"You make me very happy Renilein. I want to bring you only the good things in life."

He lay on his back, put his hands behind his head and said, "Friedrich Schiller wrote something for this occasion, little Reni--it's from Ode to Joy:

> "Who that height of bliss had proved
> Once a friend of friends to be,
> Who had won a maid beloved
> Join us in our jubilee
> Who so holds a heart in keeping
> One in all the world-his own
> Who has failed, let him with weeping
> From our fellowship begone!
> All the mighty globe containeth
> Homage to compassion pay!
> To the stars she leads the way
> Where, unknown, the God reigneth."

I stretched my hand toward Volker--he held it and kissed my fingertips. "Promise me we shall always be together."

47

"We can promise each other many things, Volker, but life brings unexpected plans. I want you to know I'd rather be with you than anyone else. I do love you but I need more time."

"I'll be patient because I love you so much. The right time will come for us to marry. In the meantime, you must meet my father. He will love you too. He is very lonely and my love for you has made me understand the loneliness Father feels without my Mother."

I thought of Karl-Heinz and my promise to him. I knew I had to write to him of my decision to marry Volker.

During the rest of the summer I heard many more poems by Schiller since Volker knew them by heart. When we walked along the Mulde River bank to pick wildflowers, he shouted all those beautiful thoughts to me. Oh those were joyous hours together.

Fall came and during October, the month to celebrate the Russian Revolution, a large party was scheduled for hospital personnel. It was to take place in the Wiesen Dance Hall.

The head Nurse assigned me to work on the night of the event. Director Rudolf, however, asked me to play my accordion for group singing during intermission.

"Sorry, I have duty that night. I cannot be there."

He was taken aback, but not for long. "But the hospital will only be staffed for emergency cases that night. Student nurses will be on duty also." He had a list of names on a board. He threw it up toward the ceiling and shouted. "Who said you'll work?"

"Doctor B_____."

"I'll see about this. Come with me," he said. I followed.

"Doctor W_____. made the duty list," said Doctor B_____. "One RN will be required for each three wards."

"But I thought student nurses would take it that night. I need Irene to play for folk singing."

Doctor B_____ handed Rudolf the phone saying, "You call her."

He took the phone and called Doctor W_____. "Hello Doctor W_____?" He hesitated. "Did you put Schwester (Sister) Irene on duty for October seventh?" He listened impatiently.

"Well, take her off!" He said and then listened.

"What do you mean there is no other nurse available?"

"Fine. Find somebody else." Silence.

"Then you will have to stay on duty yourself. I need Sister Irene." That settled it. I would now be in an even more difficult position with Doctor W_____: this one not of my making. She would not dare change Rudolf's plans.

The party was within walking distance from the hospital. Volker was my guest. Everyone was there from the hospital, from cooks to gardeners to nurses, doctors and political personnel. Who would dare not come? After the political speeches, the social activities began. We danced to the music of a four-piece band. During intermission I played my accordion and everyone sang.

A poem that had been cleverly written about almost everyone on the staff was sung solo by one of the male nurses. At the end of each verse I played the same little melody while the nurses sang, a pleasant way of poking fun at those in the Party. There is nothing better for people under tension than to sing it all out and we sure did so.

49

Volker and I danced many dances. Volker thought there was too much alcohol and I was glad he drank only moderately. Later that evening, more people had glassy eyes.

When the party was over, some thought it was too early to go home, especially since the city of Zwickau also celebrated and had a fun fair. In a mischievous mood, we confiscated the student nurses' bus and off we went. We stormed the Ferris wheel, bought tickets and filled it for a few rides. Around and around we wheeled, laughing and singing to the accompaniment of the four-piece band who had joined our party. The people around us thought they ought to join in and pretty soon there was a lot of disorder. I feared the authorities might be called in soon, some people already were talking about it.

When our merry making reached its peak the police arrived. They found out who we were and where we were from and said, "The fireworks are over" and "you must all go home now. Break it up, break it up!" There was some scuffling, but in general it was good natured and peaceful. "We'll file an official complaint with your administration in the morning." Home we went in our shabby old bus, singing all the way.

Two months passed and I spent the Christmas of 1951 with Volker and his father, Herr Rainer Hofmann. They lived in a two-room apartment which they had tidied up all by themselves. Everything was clean and orderly but also nicely decorated. Volker had even brought a Christmas tree. His father was able to buy a few bottles of red wine which we heated with spices. We joked as we decorated the tree. Earlier, they had done some bartering to have a rabbit for our Christmas feast. I helped in the preparations and provided some small trimmings to make our dinner more festive.

It was a bright night as Volker and I walked over fresh fallen snow to church. The stars sparkled in a velvet sky and the snow glistened in pools of light from the lights coming out of the windows of homes. Greetings were exchanged with friends as we entered the church. Both of our faces glowed with happiness. "It's wonderful to have you celebrate Christmas mass with me," he whispered in my ear during the service.

Christmas service was very festive and I was surprised to see such a friendly old pastor conducting the service. Although Volker was of Catholic faith, and though in Saxony almost everyone was Lutheran, he enjoyed the service.

Volker talked about having a special audience with his pastor. "I am worried that I might lose you, Renilein." His face clouded for a moment. "I would like to have his blessing for both of us."

We made an appointment with the Pastor and Volker walked with me to the train station. I only had a four-stop ride to Wiesenburg so I promised to return in the morning to continue our Christmas celebration.

On Christmas day, Volker read poems by his favorite author, Friedrich Schiller. We talked about the poems and stories and he explained those things that I did not understand. I learned many things I could never have known from books alone.

Volker had a very close relationship with his father. They were good friends, not just father and son. Herr Hofmann, with his distinguished white hair and bright friendly eyes, was as handsome as

51

Volker and he seemed to like me right away. Little things seemed to be as important to him as big things. He had a proverb for every situation.

The day after Christmas, Volker and his father escorted me on a friendly walk through town. They exchanged cheery greetings as they lifted their hats to friends. We ended our day in the Rathskeller drinking chicory and beer.

We discussed our future, where we might live and that Father WOULD live with us. His father laughed and said, "Thank you, you two."

"In a few months we'll have to give our *aufgebot*, Reni. You must go with me to make the arrangements. I'll be so proud to declare to the world we intend to marry."

"Too bad my family cannot come to City Hall and read our *aufgebot*," I said. "Can't you just see our names posted in the glass box for everyone to see? Maybe one of your ex-girlfriends will protest," I teased.

We all laughed and made more jokes about it. I loved Volker yet I had a strong feeling of apprehension that I could not understand. Perhaps my fears were a distant echo from the past war or maybe, we might say something to the wrong person and they would stop us. I surely hoped I was wrong.

On New Year's Day, 1952, Volker went home with me to see Mama and the rest of the family. Everyone was there, the boys with their girlfriends and me with Volker.

Mama was obviously pleased with Volker and he loved her too, calling her "Mama" just as I did. The boys all slept together in one room. Mama and I heard their friendly talk and laughter long after we went to bed.

Claus and Christine were anxious to tell me about school. Claus wanted to become a photographer, specializing in portraits and maybe later to even work for a magazine, with a big studio. What a dreamer he was.

"He has plenty of time to dream," Mama said. "But even if we had the money, the stores do not have cameras."

Christine was eager to explain, "We have to keep our desks clean at school. There are no people to clean up after us. We help by cleaning the floors around our desks."

"We get grades for that too," Claus chimed in.

"Yes, Irene, we do everything that Ernst Taehlmann said we must do." Christine, now seven, told me of her new philosophy of life. "We remind each other to do our homework every day and to get everything right."

I knew Ernst Taehlmann was some past leader of the Communist party and his self discipline doctrine was accepted in all ways of life. He was born in 1886 and died as a political prisoner in a concentration camp in 1944, becoming a Communist hero and martyr.

There was a policy that if a child had a special talent, something that was really outstanding, it must be developed. The child might be an important person later on, for the good and profit of the State, of course.

Christine's statements about school indicated things were orderly and that children wanted to obey their teachers.

"Mama, Claus and Christine are evidently getting good basic education. I can see homework requires concentration but what about politics?"

"They start learning that from kindergarten until they are old. It never stops. There are older children though, who are included in adult planning meetings. They listen to discussions on communism and our country's economic plans. By the time they are 14 and 16 they are working up to 12 hours a week as apprentices on factory assembly lines and other places.

"Children are taught that the work must be done perfectly because everything belongs to the State. If the State loses, everyone loses. That statement is repeated often."

"Why are they pushing such young children into the factories?"

"To replace the adults who were killed in the war and those who ran away into West Germany when they began accepting them over there. They can increase production and save money when they place children in jobs and reward them with grades. Wages are unimportant, money does not buy much here. We still stand in line for everything for our daily needs. Claus is feeling the stress now. Christine is too young to feel it yet."

"But Mama, if the children get this vocational training now, will there be enough jobs for them?"

"Teachers have the responsibility of directing children into jobs the State needs filled. For example, if the State wants more waiters or waitresses for their State-owned restaurants, the teacher must persuade the girl or boy to become just that. When the Five Year Plan demands 100 cooks, 100 boys and girls must become cooks. The five year plan must be fulfilled."

"There is no real educational freedom. They are being completely indoctrinated into Communist philosophy and their relationship to the State." I felt much bitterness about this injustice.

Mama continued, "Every day they must look their teachers straight in the eye and tell them how much they love the socialist State. They are taught to answer 'We must not be influenced by western radio.'"

"I don't like it, we will never be a free people!" I said.

While riding the train back to Wiesen, Volker told me of his frequent hikes along the border near Hirschberg and of going over the border to Hof during the hard years after the war.

"The real freedom is in the West, you and I both know this, Irene. I have helped some of my friends find their way across the border. Their letters tell of much better conditions on the western side."

We both agreed that our families kept us from going into West Germany. Father Hofmann, as I called Volker's father, was much too frail to take a chance like that, and if we were caught, he would never survive a day in prison.

We returned to our separate jobs, seeing each other as often as possible. My resentment towards the Party increased. When the Party decided that extra work must be done they came around with a list for everyone to sign. We called it the "Voluntary Must List."

We were asked to work on our day off each week and to contribute the day's wage to a Culture Palace being built in Chemnitz, near Rabenstein Hospital. Doctors, nurses and other personnel begrudged putting their signatures to this agreement.

Not wanting to sacrifice my free days to this project, I went to the Party Office.

"Ah, Comrade Irene, what brings you here?" I never did like that "comrade" stuff.

"I need my free days--" The man at the desk arose, took me by the shoulders and turned me around before I could say more.

"It was nice seeing you," he said as he walked me toward the door. He whispered, "Don't get yourself into trouble." Then he was louder as he gently pushed me out the door saying, "See you, Comrade."

He knew what I wanted. He also knew that if I objected it could get me into trouble and would ruin my life: no job, no pay, no privileges or rights and eventually a labor camp. It was a ritual that happened all the time.

I signed away my free days.

I must explain our pay days. We were paid once each month and always in cash. We were paid in the dining hall where tables were arranged in a U-pattern. After receiving our pay at one end of the "U" we proceeded along the other tables to pay back to persons representing about six or more different government organizations: *Freie Deutsche Jugeno* in short FDJ, (Free German Youth), *Gewerkschaft*, (Union), Cultural development, German Soviet Friendship, *Frauenbewegung* (Women's Organizations), and the Communist Party occupied two tables. The latter collected from their members only.

Everybody resented this immediate cash handout and there was no way to avoid them. Needless to say, taxes and other deductions were already taken away. We used to say, payday was like having a whole tree and cutting a little toy out of it, and being given the toy as your pay.

The first day of May is the Workers' Day in East Germany, a day of big parades and programmed demonstrations. Those who parade are the people.

Literally every citizen of both Wiesen and Wiesenburg, from the young school children to the hospital staff, were required to parade. Therefore, there were no onlookers. It always seemed strange to me, whenever we had to get into one of those parades. This was not a dress-up affair; everyone wore their working clothes. Doctors disliked participating in this parade, especially the surgeons. But there could be no excuses, they had to appear and walk.

A few old folks stood on the sidewalk watching us going by, along with some people with drinking water and first aid supplies we saw on the way. I wished they also had first aid people on the other occasions when we had longer parades. We paraded downhill from Wiesen to the railroad station by the Mulde River in Wiesenburg, and back up the hill to Wiesen. It took a few hours. Most of us thought it was senseless. Following this exhibition of the working people, everyone went back to their duties.

BERLIN - 1952

News of the *Jugendfestspiele* (Youth Festival) to be held in East Berlin came to us in the late spring of 1952. As specified by the State, most young people working in our hospital were required to go to Berlin for this event. I had other plans.

"You're asking for trouble, Irene, if you refuse to go," Rudi the Cultural Director said. "We will put you on the list anyway. You are going."

The purpose of amassing the youth of East Germany was to demonstrate to the world the unity and happiness of the Socialist State. I loved my work but I didn't think I should have to march in Berlin to prove it. But I had to go.

Some older workers were very enthusiastic, but they were not in the youth program. They had never been in Berlin, so they alone wanted to participate. They had to pay their own way, and those enthusiastic people who were so happy in Communist East Germany went right into West Berlin and stayed there.

The Youth Festival was scheduled to last for several weeks. Twenty-two nurses from our hospital were assigned to go on different days. The passes came and I knew that I must go. "You'll be going with a large group. Be at the square in Aue at nine in the morning. Go into the town square and wait," I was told.

Since early morning, we had been sitting on top of our bags which held only a toothbrush and enough clothes for a few days. We waited in the square. Hours passed. Slowly the square filled with about 2000 young people, mostly girls, with the exception of a few boys' units. Most of the males had gathered at another town square. Almost all of them were wearing uniforms, black skirts and deep blue blouses, the dress of the FDJ (Free German Youth). *What an ironic name*, I thought.

By late afternoon, though thirsty and hungry, we were told to stand four abreast. After being counted, we marched around the square still carrying our luggage.

We now numbered more than 3000. We were counted again and grouped under leaders. They allowed us to stop marching and rest, but we could not leave the area for any reason. Like a herd of cattle, we stood when they whistled, we sat when they whistled and we sang when they felt we should do so. When we were ordered to march again, we were to sing the Communist songs. I had not learned them and did not know the words. The leaders saw that I was not singing and shouted angrily, "Sing! Sing!" I moved my lips to the songs.

Everyone watched everyone else and the leaders watched all of us. There were no restroom facilities and no food or drink. I wondered how they would move us to Berlin. No train could hold so many. The answer came--we were crowded into boxcars, fifty to each car including luggage.

"This will be a short trip," I heard, and it was.

We arrived in Oberschlema one half hour later and got off the train. Constant whistle-blowing and shouting of orders took me back to the time when I was ten years old and the BDM Hitler Youth marched during the Nazi time. The girls were enthusiastic members of the FDJ. "*Give them some power and they go crazy,*" I thought. I had nothing in common with them.

We stood at attention in lines and it took hours to get the 3000 people organized. Roll calls became more frequent. They ordered us to count ourselves and to shout the numbers loudly. Those who were slow got a jab in the ribs. If one turned up missing there was a search and the group leader got minus points which made her unhappy and mean. Those girls could really blow the whistle and bellow orders right into our faces.

We stood at attention and saw the sun go down. Darkness came, and as usual there were no street lights. At the spot where they loaded up many people during the festival, the Party had many large head lights installed on high masts. We still stood, waiting for something.

That day was nothing but military drills and no food or water. It was no use looking for a bathroom, there were none, period. Since we had to sing one song after another and we kept repeating them, I began to pick up some of the songs. When my mouth became very dry I just moved my lips. I longed for a drink of water. I wanted to run away, but there were dozens of leaders watching us under glaring search lights which kept sweeping up and down the lines. Group leaders were watched by other leaders.

Finally some men and women arrived. They were not the FDJ but the Communist Party people. Nobody smiled, no friendly faces, just big mouths shouting orders. Roll call again and again.

It was ridiculous. I thought they were waiting for an order to board the train. Something began to happen-one could sense that some VIP had arrived. Leaders gave their reports.

With no food or water all day, I was not too uncomfortable about the lack of restroom facilities. Some of the girls looked miserable and ready to cry. We were again marched group after group toward the boxcars.

"Anyone needing to go must use the bushes along the tracks. No more than five girls at a time and only with your leaders. Leave your luggage where it is," yelled out group leaders.

Although urgently necessary, the order seemed unbelievable. I imagined three thousand people trying go into the bushes at the same time and felt ill. There was no chance to run away since the searchlights moved constantly along the tracks where we were standing. The bushes were so small and sparse, one did not need glasses to see what was going on.

As this necessary but tiresome episode took place, the odor of urine nauseated me. Again we lined up in front of the boxcars.

Several Russian officers on their way to the train station were watching us. One of them began to curse and make repeated gestures with his hand across his neck as though he wanted to slit our throats. When we had to sing again, he became especially angry. He worked himself into such a frenzy by his cursing that it became obvious to all who saw him how deeply he hated the Germans. The men he was with told him to cool it, but had he been alone, he probably would have crashed into our lines. Some of the girls began to show signs of fear, evidently remembering those times of rape following the war.

Group leaders were trying not to show their own fear. They shouted for us to ignore what was taking place and to get into the boxcars. I watched another officer hold his drunken friend back and try to smile at us pretending like his friend's behavior was a joke. It was not. While the Russian officer cursed, we marched past singing about German-Soviet friendship and how happy we would be to fulfill their next Five-Year Plan.

We climbed into the freight cars again, 50 girls to a car. We sat on a very dirty floor and our legs were stepped on as we struggled to find a place to rest. When we pushed somebody, somebody pushed back. There were absolutely too many of us in such a cramped place. The doors slammed shut. It was suffocating and nauseating. I felt I wouldn't be able to make it until morning.

"I want air! Air!" I screamed. In total darkness I felt nothing but bodies, no wall, nothing to lean on but bodies!

Some girls succeeded in opening the door not more than a foot wide on the other side of the car, letting in some much needed air. Luckily there was an iron bar so no one could be pushed out, but it was attached in such a way that the door could not be opened wider. Since it was the first trip to Berlin for most of the girls, the excitement helped them endure the suffocation and fatigue.

The train was rolling fast now. I figured the trip to Berlin would take about half the night. However, we rolled east to Bautzen, which is the home of the largest penitentiary in East Germany. From there we rolled farther east toward the Polish border. We stopped in stations for hours as more cars were added.

During the entire trip we were allowed to get off once and then only to use the bushes along the train embankment; always we were under the watchful eyes of our leaders. As our fatigue grew we lay like sardines, trying to rest but too tired to complain. I never slept in such a terrible position in my life and it really upset me. I know I slept on top of somebody's body and somebody's head and bodies were lying on top of me. When one person moved the others awoke and moved also.

As daylight came I was lying on the floor wedged tightly between two bodies. I tried to make my way to the door for a breath of fresh air but found others there before me. They were lying on top of one another straining for fresh air.

The cool morning air revived us. We were now at the Polish border. We saw guards all along the train embankment. They wore Russian uniforms and had machine guns strapped on their backs. They looked at us and we looked at them, but nobody made a sound. As we passed small stations, large signs and posters carried the names of the Polish leaders. So much propaganda. We would fulfill the Five Year Plan.

Hours later we arrived at the edge of Berlin. When the first houses came into sight and people appeared on the streets, the entire train full of girls and boys started screaming and singing. If one sings, there is no time to complain or even talk.

The train stopped once or twice to unload passengers. Schools were recessed to provide us with lodging in the classrooms. Around noon we arrived tired, hungry and dirty at our destination. We were unloaded and marched, four abreast, singing every weary foot of the way from the train to the appointed school building.

"After you are assigned a room you may have the rest of the day off. Tomorrow we march," shouted the leader.

Classroom floors were covered with straw for sleeping. We were given a cup of chicory, a piece of salami and one piece of dark sourdough bread. I drank the chicory and put the bread and salami in my suitcase. I wanted to clean up before eating.

Unable to find a washroom in the huge building, I was told to go into the courtyard.

There in the open were about twenty little water faucets along a pipe. Under these was a long shallow trough which was to be our sink. The water was ice cold and I was angry.

"How am I supposed to wash myself? This is crazy!" No one heard me.

I looked up at the numerous windows in the four story school building to see many observers laughing. To my surprise I saw one of the male nurses from Wiesen looking out of the window, enjoying the view. That did it!

"I want the man out of that window immediately! Look at those stupid girls. They have actually undressed to the waist to wash in this place. This makes me sick!"

No one listened. I found an empty marmalade bucket and filled it with water. I looked around and saw at least a dozen outhouses lined up one next to the other. They were homemade with more space inside than the American standard size ones have. The toilet locker

64

was unsatisfactory but gave privacy just the same. After washing I came out, brushed my teeth at a faucet and then went upstairs to eat.

After eating I found the room where the male nurses were ogling the girls below.

"I'll report this stupid behavior when I get back!"

Their arrogant statement of "we are in charge here" brought an immediate argument. What followed convinced each of us the other person was wrong. I left.

My clothes were badly wrinkled and I was told to "iron them at the home of the school custodian across the street."

While waiting my turn for the iron, I listened to the custodian's wife warn us about the evils of West Berlin and West Germany in general.

"If anyone is caught out of line they will be punished severely. Better not go near the West at all. We want you to go and see our war memorials here in Berlin. Here, I'll show you how to get there." She was really laying it on us. The girls, ranging in age from 16 to 24, were smiling and winking.

"Yes, Frau Mueller. No, Frau Mueller. We know, Frau Mueller." To further emphasize her warnings, a loudspeaker in the school courtyard blared continual threats to anyone who might consider going into West Berlin.

In spite of these warnings, I wanted to see West Berlin if at all possible. As I walked toward the U-Bahn station I saw girls crowding around some street-side stands. The girls were walking away with large pieces of red fruit. Curious, I bought some. It was our first taste of watermelon. "They were brought in from Russia for the youth festival," I was told. It sure was a welcome treat to go with our salami and dark bread.

As I approached the dividing line between East and West Berlin, the number of police rapidly increased. Each group of four German policemen was accompanied by two Russian patrolmen with their ever-ready machine guns.

Near the ticket counter by the U-Bahn (metro), a middle aged couple was arguing loudly with two policemen. I and several others watched this argument develop into a scuffle. When the woman attempted to help her husband, a swarm of police hurried to control them.

While they marched this couple away, I walked to the ticket counter, purchased my ticket and boarded the U-Bahn. My heart pounded loudly as I seated myself in the car. I smiled at several people in an effort to hide my fear. Then the door closed and the train moved toward West Berlin.

No one checked my ID when I rose to leave the train in West Berlin. I smiled again at a woman leaving the train with me but did not relax until I arrived at the Amerika Haus (America House), situated near Lehndorf Square. America House was a center where programs, books, magazines and movies told about life in the United States.

During those early days the wall between East and West Berlin was yet to be built. However, the trains were stopped at random intervals every day by East German police and Russian Soldiers intent on seeking out and arresting anyone who did not have their ID with them or who did not give a good enough explanation as to why they were on the train going into West Berlin. If anyone could not prove that they lived in or around Berlin, they were suspected of defecting and were immediately and brutally arrested.

At the Amerika Haus I watched a movie about life in the United States. It was about an hour long and I watched it twice. It showed farmers harvesting wheat with their big machines and I saw their homes, their highways, and the cars they drove. They did not lose their homes in the war. Oh, what a peaceful life it must be. *How lucky people were to be born in the United States*, I thought. I wondered though if they realized it.

I asked the lady who worked at American House how one could go to the United States. She smiled and asked if I had relatives or friends there.

"No," I answered.

"Well," she said. "Then it would be very difficult to get there."

I understood, of course. America seemed like another world.

I spent all afternoon watching movies and daydreaming about people who were my age, living in the USA. As darkness came, I walked along the Ku-Damm, just as I had done on my vacation trip. I was fascinated by the large, lighted letters that rolled from one end of a long sign to the other to display the latest news. Expensive new dresses and shoes were offered for sale in store windows. Outside the Sarotti Chocolate store, the smell of chocolate was intoxicating. Just standing in front of this store and taking it all in was heaven. Stores like that were always full of customers. People were buying the finest chocolate pralines by the pound, yet we back home were not able to buy even one ounce of anything half as good.

Also on display were newspapers, hundreds of different titled magazines, and all kinds of paperback novels which filled multiple Kiosks. It certainly was another world and definitely not a socialist one.

I fervently wished to stay in West Berlin, but everyone I loved was in East Germany. Not only that, but there was no one in the West with whom I could live. I did not have my birth certificate with me, or any other important papers. I was not yet ready to go.

I heard great shouting and singing coming over the loudspeakers from East Berlin. The East and West sometimes had shouting matches. I was certain I recognized the voices coming from East Berlin. They would be the voices of the demonstration there. *Tomorrow*, I thought, *I will again be a part of it.*

It was dark when I got off the U-Bahn in East Berlin. Street lights were dim and far apart and it was after the hour I was supposed to be in. I entered the school through a back door and slipped into the classroom where I was assigned. The floor was covered with straw. Once again too many girls in one room, and somebody's feet kicked my head when I laid down. Another girl had picked up my food rations for the next day, salami and bread again.

"Everybody has to be asleep early," she whispered as she handed me the food. "We have a long day ahead."

I washed up and was informed that I was being reported. I saw on the paper "possibly been in West Berlin."

"You will be dealt with when you get home," said a leader.

We were awakened at 4 a.m., and we were told to get up and *Schnell! Schnell! (*Hurry! Hurry!). My eyes weren't open yet and my head was ringing from all the orders being given. Outside it was dark. In the building the light was still dim throughout the entire building and everybody was stumbling over everyone else. Luckily I got my teeth brushed, but that was all. Once dressed, we lined up with no time allowed for anything else. We were crowded into old WWII army trucks and even when we thought it was full they kept pushing in more people. Those who had to stand must have had a very hard time. Although I conquered a seat, somebody was sitting on top of me and my legs were cramped. We were driven to some open railroad tracks with no station around and marched into waiting boxcars. We had no idea where we were. As much as it could be seen through holes in the boxcar, we saw the sun rising. Then the train moved, stopped, there were more people loaded, and slowly we moved forward again. We heard orders shouted and a male voice bellowed, "Make those slowpokes move! *Schnell! Schnell!"*

As the sun began to warm us, we ate our bread and salami with nothing to drink to help the salty salami down. Somebody said, "This is the famous Hungarian salami. Enjoy it! You won't see that stuff again."

The train stopped and the unloading began. The leaders were hoarse from shouting and my only wish was to get away. We were marched four abreast for a good mile, then stopped for another roll call. The leaders seemed excited, someone was missing. We stayed in line and waited. Eleven o'clock came, still we stood four abreast in a populated neighborhood. There were apartment buildings, old and used up, and still we saw no pedestrians. "They don't want to have anything to do with us," someone said. We had no watches but it must have been noon when instructions were given to tens of thousands of us on how to march and who to follow into an enormous stadium. The lines of marchers stretched for many blocks.

People arrived wearing uniforms and folk art dresses. They must have been the ones who danced and performed the propaganda words for the movie camera. Television stations were not in our country yet.

An hour before our march began, heavy flagpoles with large red flags were passed out.

"Two girls will share a flag. They are heavy so divide your time," blasted a voice over the loudspeaker. "These flags must be held upright at all times!"

This tops it all, I thought. I sensed we were in for a long walk. Life came into the lines and the front rows began to move. We followed, slowly at first, then faster.

"Don't get behind. Keep up. Take longer steps, hurry."

We took turns carrying those bloody red flags.

"Hold it higher!" my leader barked.

"It's very heavy," we complained.

As we were marching, papers came showering out of the sky. I was sure they were leaflets from the West, but with both hands full and that red flag in front of me flapping in my face, I could not get one. I handed the flag to my neighbor. I just had to have one of those leaflets. They were lying on the ground and we were trampling on them.

"Don't you dare pick them up," warned a loud voice. "Anyone who picks one up gets severe punishment."

70

One fluttered down in front of me and I grabbed it. There was an immediate scuffle. Raging with anger, the leader burst through the line and ripped it out of my hands.

"You're on the black list now," my fellow flag-bearer said as my name was written down. I still did not know what was written on the paper. I was thinking more about that than the expected punishment I was to get.

We reached the area in front of the big stage where government leaders stood smiling and waving to us. Those in front started their dances as we waved the red flags and marched around the stage. Everybody was singing.

The trumpets blared, red flags billowed back and forth as the inner circle of girls spelled out their propaganda messages of "Love" to the Party officials. It was an enormous demonstration. Some girls seemed to be in a state of ecstasy as they acted out this fantasy of movement and song; others just smiled. All the while there were leaders among us telling us how many steps to take. Go left, go right, move.

We passed the flags to the line behind us, took each others' hands and walked, and then changed our hands to another line. This worked out pretty well and must have looked organized from where the officials were watching us. Tens of thousands of us moved constantly to the shouted orders of leaders. We sang and walked a folk dance. It was a sea of people. I had never seen so many people in one place. I did not know there were so many left after the bloodletting of the war. We were all young and being told, "You are the future of the country."

From the expression on the faces of those reviewing our actions, we were making an impressive presentation.

After a long time we moved toward the exit. Our voices were strong and I was sure this was the sound I heard the day before while I was in West Berlin. As our screams rent the air, mine was not for communism. I screamed in despair to get out of this place and into the sweet freedom of the West. In my mind I saw the golden wheat fields waving in the breeze beneath the blue sky. I saw farmers harvesting grain in the United States of America and wished that my brothers, Mama and Volker with his father could all be on such a farm.

Outside the stadium it was chaos. Nobody knew where they belonged and I had no idea where I was. Where were the leaders? Did they not know that not one of us knew this part of Berlin? I saw streets with rubble on both sides and in between, stands were set up to give out ice-water. We were very thirsty. Much further up the street there were signs telling people which district they belonged to and how to get back to their school. Boxcars were waiting to take us back, but now that everything was less organized, ten horses couldn't get me back into those boxcars. I chose to find my way back on my own and other people had the same idea. Three or four of us went together, still in a festive mood, we walked past entire blocks that had been destroyed by the bombs. As I stopped to get a cup of cold water, I heard my name being called.

"Sister Irene, Schwester Irene!"

I turned around and saw a familiar face from Wiesen. "What school are you in? Now that we are all going home tomorrow, we should see some of Berlin in the evening." I was much too tired to think about going anywhere, although sitting in that schoolhouse listening to orders until tomorrow was not very inviting either.

As I reached my district and eventually my school, it was late afternoon. Most of the girls were out; everybody wanted to see something of Berlin. After all, so far we had seen nothing but the stadium. I met the young people from Wiesen, and off we went. One of them knew her way around, and she led us to a streetcar that took us to a different section of the city. There, the five of us entered a coffee house, elegantly decorated and full of people. A band was playing both popular Eastern and Western music. We found a table and ordered something to drink. I was aghast, *so these are the East Berlin places where the West Germans come to have a good time for little money*. People were well-dressed in comparison to us; for them, money was no object.

I remembered Linda's cousin telling us that they went dancing in East Berlin, because here, they only paid a fifth of what it would cost to go out in West Berlin.

When they saw all of us girls coming in, the music played and one of the West Berliners started an impromptu floor show singing and dancing. Another one followed and he was clowning around our table, making faces while he played the saxophone. We laughed and clapped, calling out "Encore."

They liked this and clowned even more bringing about much laughter. I hadn't laughed so much for a long time. This was good fun and I began to relax after the long and tiring youth demonstration.

A half a dozen husky guys came in and looked things over for a while. They seemed like real bullies to me. Our fun waned.

73

Suddenly, for no apparent reason, they came across the room like a thunderstorm and towered over our's and other people's tables. The band stopped. Everyone got nervous and the air was tense.

"Is this human culture?" one of the bullies asked us girls. "Aren't those guys humiliating the human body?"

We all felt frightened at seeing his ugly beer-smelling face so close to ours.

"They are the decadent West!" He leaned over the table even more, as if he wanted to strike some of us. Was it because we had clapped so enthusiastically? The young men who had done the clowning were looking sober now. We sensed the tension. One spark and the whole place would be a shambles with someone getting hurt. We didn't want a fight. How unnecessary this all was, but those bullies had come in to start a fight. Stammering something, we all got up and left as quickly as we could walk. Then the fight did start, and we could hear cursing, bodies hitting wood, crashing furniture and shouting. We started to run. Having our fun interrupted, we felt tired and caught a street car back to our school quarters.

I had had enough of all this and hoped to get a few hours of sleep before the long journey started home again. When I went to sleep on the straw that night I vowed to myself I would never go to such an event again.

Long before dawn the next morning whistles pierced the air, and it was "Up and out! On the double!" Another trainload of youth would be arriving soon and the program would repeat itself to puff up the self-important feelings of the State politicians. Once on the train, the girls sang like crazy. They seemed glad to be going home. The leaders, wanting more room in their car, stuffed extra girls in ours. It was unbearable.

I estimated six to eight hours of travel time and again I was wrong. I managed to keep my place near the door, which was opened just a crack for air. It made breathing a little easier. But for some, it was pretty bad. We were given salami and dark bread again, with nothing to drink. Of course, we had no toilet facilities. The salty salami made us all very thirsty.

Long into the night, after the train had been diverted many times, we stopped and were allowed to get off for a drink at the faucets near the tracks on some deserted small railroad station. Several Russian soldiers were guarding the station while others were sitting around on the ground.

When they saw hundreds of girls pouring out of the boxcars, those soldiers got excited at seeing us.

Everyone was headed toward some water faucets and the leaders were shouting at us to hurry. We had to cup our hands to hold a few swallows of water and people dripped over each other.

I boarded the train toward the last so I could keep my place near the door for fresh air. When I reached up to climb into the boxcar, a soldier grabbed me around the waist. I screamed as he clapped his hand over my mouth. His rough hand smelled of garlic, and it suffocated me. Of course, no leaders were in sight. Several girls reached out, got hold of me and pulled while kicking the Russian. He filled the air with curses as I was hauled to safety. The train pulled out and we rolled the rest of the night.

At dawn, the sign "*Zwickau*" was a welcome sight. I grabbed my bag and reported to leave. I was told I would soon hear from the authorities as I left the boxcar.

MISSTEP

I was anxious to tell Volker about West Berlin and my desire to permanently cross the border. On my next day off I met Volker by the Mulde River Bridge. Volker's long embrace told me he had missed me. I had not forgotten how blue his eyes were.

We walked along the grassy farmland and up the gentle slope which soon took us to where no village or farmhouses were in sight.

"It is good to be here with you again, Volker."

"Please don't ever leave me again," he said, holding me in a warm embrace.

"I was only gone five days. But I have so much to tell you."

The summer air was sweet as we walked hand in hand up another slope and came to a pond. Placing our picnic basket and my accordion on the ground, we spread out a blanket and sat down to rest.

"I went into West Berlin, Volker. I saw wonderful things; I learned much about America. I wish we could go there. I want to live in a free country. More than anything else I want to be free. This political pressure depresses me."

He took my hand and looked at me for a long time. "Irene, there is no real future for us here, we both know that. We could plan to leave secretly, but what about your mother and my father? They depend upon us. We have no relatives in West Germany. It will not be easy to leave our families behind."

"I am going to try to get Mama to go but I'm not sure she will leave."

"The time isn't right yet, Irene. We must wait a little longer."

"How long? Until it is too late?" I shouted. "I thought you knew. The Communists have closed off the border between East and West Germany permanently. Roads are cut off and railroad tracks are interrupted. Barbed wire fences are being erected now all along the border. This is only the beginning. Soon, they will lay mines, you know; they shoot to kill at people, we'll never get out. Never!" I cried. But I knew he was right.

We sat there and he tried to comfort me and he tried to make a joke. But my desire for freedom would not be stilled. Instead of talking anymore, we opened the picnic basket and started to eat.

After a while, I picked up my accordion and began to play. We both sang "Nun Adieu Du Mein Lieb' Heimatland."

After the last words ". . . from the green downstream and stony height, I salute you now, this final time, You, my native land, good bye." Volker lay back and said, "If I could embroider that white cloud with wings, I'd spread it under your feet and we'd fly into West Germany right now, my darling."

I loved Volker with all my heart, but I felt like a bird beating my wings against a wire cage trying to get out.

I took a few days leave and went home. Soon after I arrived I asked Mama why she looked so worried.

"I had a terrible dream, Irene. I dreamt that you escaped to the West and we were never able to see each other again."

"Mama, if we are going to leave, now is the time to do it. It is getting more dangerous all the time. The sooner the better."

Ortwin put a newspaper on the table and pointed, "Look, there are articles like this every day about *volksfeinde* (enemies of the people) who try to escape and get caught."

"You have to be bold, look them in the eye and smile," I said. "If we are going to get out, we must do it now. I believe the U-Bahn in Berlin is the safest way to go."

"What about luggage?" Mama asked.

"We could take no luggage. That would only bring suspicion. The train system is under Russian control and if they even suspect someone from East Germany wants to get into West Berlin, they stop the train and check IDs. If you run, they don't hesitate to shoot. People get arrested all the time and are sent to labor camps or Bautzen."

"We cannot risk this for our entire family." Mama said. "It must get better soon. It can't go on like this."

I knew it would be dangerous for all of us to try to go together. We would be much more likely to be stopped. While I had learned enough of the Berlin dialect to purchase a ticket on the U-Bahn. I also knew that the Saxony dialect would be a dead giveaway for every member of the family. I dared not press this matter any further.

The next morning the door bell rang and I opened the door to see Herr Viehstig, our Culture Director, and some other Party people from Wiesen. Shocked, I gestured for them to come in. What in the world could they want? I was soon to find out.

"You behaved disgracefully in Berlin, Irene," Viehstig accused.

The blood drained from my face. I felt cold and shaky. He went on. "You did not know our national anthem and you refused to carry the flag." He went on reading from a list. "You tried to pick up an enemy leaflet and you were seen in West Berlin. Those are very serious accusations and you must be dealt with." I was stricken by these charges which, for the most part, were true. How did they know I had been in West Berlin?

"You are suspended from duty until further notice."

"I cannot go back to work?" It was incredulous.

"Not until we have decided what to do with you. You are to stay here. Report to me in three days." He was pretty sure that I wasn't going anywhere. The whole country was a jail and he knew I would be there in three days. They left.

"There is no chance to go into West Berlin now. You will be watched." Mama was as stunned as I was. I spent three agonizing days in grief and fear. I knew this would now make my file look as if I was a criminal. In a dictatorship there exists a file on every citizen from birth on, and any misstep, however trivial, is recorded and can bring charges with permanent consequences.

I returned to Wiesen and learned I wouldn't be permitted to return to work.

"You shall work at hard labor in the uranium mines." For how long was not clear. Gretl was angry and sad.

I immediately became one of the miners who traveled to Niederschlema and Aue on the train. Wearing a mining suit and rubber boots, the same work was required of both men and women. I first became a *radiometrist*. Carrying a Geiger counter, I walked both along the slope and underground in search of uranium. When the Geiger counter buzzed with rapid clicking, indicating uranium was present, those places were marked for later digging. They would dig for the ore until the Geiger counter could detect no more. This was an easy job, but unfortunately it lasted only a few days and then I was reassigned.

Lorries brought heavy pitchblende out of the mine where they were put onto elevators and raised three or four stories high. There they dumped their contents onto a mountain of black dirt and a chute carried the pitchblende down in stages. The second stage of the chute had an opening where men and women stood on a platform separating large rocks out of the fine dirt with shovels. When the black dirt thundered down in large quantities they could not remove all the rocks quick enough. Another platform, at a lower level, held men and women whose job it was to divert the remaining rocks out of the pitchblende. Chutes then funneled the pitchblende out onto a hill where open freight cars were pulled in to be filled.

I worked inside the freight cars with three others, mostly men. We shoveled the heavy dirt into the corners and sides so the car would fill evenly. Even though we used large shovels, if we did not shovel quickly enough, we would be covered by the pitchblende.

After a car was filled we jumped off quickly because it would roll away and the next car would come into its' place. We climbed swiftly into the next car and repeated the fast shoveling. Full cars left immediately for Russia as everything ordered by Russia was done rapidly and without question.

I worked frantically to keep my corner of the car filled evenly. If one of the work team was slow it brought quick criticism from the others. Workers not completing their work quota were docked on food rations.

Huge blisters formed on my hands the first day, but I kept shoveling the heavy black dirt. Once the supervisor jumped into the car to help me finish my share, then he yelled, "Get off!"

The car was moving before I could recover the shovel he left behind. The car was gaining speed!

"Jump!" someone yelled.

I did and my blistered hands stung as I hit the ground. As I climbed up into the next car I could see that the blisters on my hands had broken.

"Hurry! Hurry! Shovel faster," the workers shouted. "Fill your shovel. They want this train loaded and on the way to Russia today."

It was each man for himself. No help was given. We worked feverishly and there was no time to look anywhere except at the hurtling black dirt. Every second counted.

Russian guards, posted in special watchtowers high above us, watched as we worked. If I had not known that I could go home that night, I would have thought I was already in a hard labor camp. I shoveled as fast as I could though my hands felt raw and I was in great pain. The broken blisters cut deep into the flesh. I felt like a person without hands. How could I go on? They were so pitiful to look at that I cried. No matter how hard I tried I could not keep up with the men. The pain in my hands became intense, beyond bearing, and they still shouted, "Hurry faster, get it done!"

I prayed, *Please, God, take me home. I have nothing more to lose on this ugly planet.*

I tried mightily to keep up my share of the shoveling but could not complete it in time. Jumping from the moving cars hurt my whole body.

Evening finally came. We picked up our special ration coupons and without having a chance to wash up, we walked, sweaty and filthy, down to Niederschlema to catch a train home. Now I understood why the miners sat on top of the train rather than inside the cars. They wanted fresh air, especially those who worked underground.

"Do you get blisters?" I asked the man sitting next to me on the train. He laughed. "Of course, and muscles too." I could see the muscles under the clothes of the people on the train. *They will survive this,* I thought, *but I won't.*

At home I took a bath and went to bed. Gretl brought me some food but I was too tired to eat much of it. She cleaned my hands, spread salve on the raw, open sores, and bandaged them. Without any effort, I fell asleep.

Next morning I felt stiff as a board. Every move hurt. I groaned with pain as I dressed, rode the train to Niederschlema, and walked up to the mines.

My shift changed every week. The mines were operated around the clock and at a back-breaking pace. I hated the night shifts when we pitched the heavy black dirt against the sides of black freight cars. I felt as though I was fighting black devils and they were winning.

I told the supervisor I could not endure the work. "I'll get the whole team behind in their quota."

"I might find you a different job but for now you get with it! We have to keep up this speed to fill the cars on time."

The miners did not talk much, everyone was too exhausted. If any slight break came, we slumped down to get some much needed rest. I was never able to keep up with the other workers, and jumping from rolling freight trains was getting difficult and extremely painful.

One evening Gretl said, "If you stay up there too long you will become sterile from the uranium. You'll never be able to have children." I had no answer for that.

As I tried to keep up, the workers said, "You're soft. Take more on your shovel. Throw faster! Make every move faster!" To me, that black dirt was as heavy as iron.

One evening Volker came to see me. He was visibly shocked to see the weight I had lost. When he saw the difficulty I had standing up straight, he sat me down and took both my hands in his. He looked at the palms of my hands which were crusted with dark calluses.

"Reni, my Reni, what are they doing to you? This is enough. Gretl, we must stop this cruelty."

"We had better get her mother to come and talk to the Party officials," Gretl said. "Irene cannot survive this work."

"You must see a doctor, Renilein," Volker said.

"Seeing a doctor is not easy, Volker. Their waiting rooms are full. You know yourself they often send the sick back to work. There are too many sick people. The doctors at the hospital who know me are afraid to request that I come back to work.

84

"I'll see what I can do," he said.

Gretl and Volker talked, and then he left. A few days later Gretl and Mama went to the Party officials but they were told that I had to learn my lesson. After many weeks I was assigned to work on a platform sorting rocks out of the pitchblende. The dirt came down with a tremendous noise. I never heard one human voice during the entire eight-hour shift. While the work was far from easy, it was less difficult than shoveling in the freight cars. We were not timed and I had a few minutes between filling boxcars.

Although given extra food ration coupons after each shift, I lost my appetite and ate very little. My arms began to feel numb. I was getting weaker and nothing interested me anymore.

"Please go to a hospital and see a doctor," Gretl begged.

Volker asked Doctor S_____ to come see me. He came one evening and after his examination he said, "You are suffering from total exhaustion. I'm going to talk to the Party people and see what I can do. This work will harm you permanently if you keep it up." Good Doctor S_____. He really wanted to help.

Sometimes I thought that all the people talking on my behalf did more harm than good. *Once winter comes I will die*, I thought. *It was just too much for me.*

One day I came home from the mines to find Father Hofmann waiting for me. He looked sad.

"What's happened?"

"They have arrested Volker."

I was stunned. "What is he accused of?"

"You won't believe this--it started with his school plays when he used to teach school. He did not put enough Party ideology into his work. He has also been accused of helping young people escape into West Germany."

A chill shot through my body as I sat down. "How can I help? What can I do?"

"He is in deep trouble." Volker's father looked beaten. "He wanted you to know."

I felt as though I was in a vice. "I feel so helpless."

"So do I. We'll have to do something, but what?" With that he left a broken man. Volker was all he had left.

Volker's sentence came quickly. He was given no chance to defend himself. There were no open trials like in a free country. No lawyer and no jury. The condemning evidence was a letter from West Germany. A grateful student sent it from West Germany to thank Volker for helping him escape.

I felt sick when I heard the news and could not get out of bed the next morning. I lost all my strength. Even my will to live seemed gone.

Party people, seeking revenge on Volker, would not allow any of us to see him. He got 15 years for spying and being an enemy of the State. In those days, just getting caught crossing the border brought 15 years or more.

A few days later the Culture Director appeared, smiling and showing off his gold tooth, which I wished to knock out. He said, "You have shown us that you can endure punishment. If you promise to behave, we will reinstate you as a nurse again. You will not work in the main hospital but in the Annex."

I was too sick to even feel relief. I showed no emotion at all but after they left, I cried because I could not talk with Volker. I remembered the blessing Volker had insisted we get in church last Christmas. I remembered how he held my hand during that blessing and how he wanted us to be together forever. It was not meant to be. Was this going to be the answer to my uneasy feelings about our love? No! I could not accept this!

I rested a few more days, then went back to work. It was good to wear a clean uniform again, but with Volker gone from my life, I felt little enthusiasm for anything.

The Annex where I was to work was located halfway down the hill between the hospital building and the railroad station. The pharmacy was located in the basement. The first floor held patients with internal illnesses. Food was delivered to patients from the main hospital.

As I approached the hospital entrance on my first day back, two of the male nurses came out of the building carrying a dead body wrapped loosely in a sheet. They threw it like a piece of wood onto a four wheeled hand wagon.

In answer to my look of surprise, one of them said, "He died one hour ago. A bad heart. We are taking him to the morgue."

"But you don't have to throw the body," I gasped.

"He doesn't feel a thing now."

"But that is not the idea." Aghast at their callousness, I said, "Don't you have any respect for the dead?"

"Wait until you are dead, Irene. They are going to use your head for a bowling ball," they said laughing. A wave of nausea filled me.

I liked working in the Annex because Party officials seldom came around, which suited me just fine. I was actually more on my own than before. After my experience in the mines I felt much more compassion toward the sick miners.

One night two miner's trains collided and we were told to expect the worst. The trains were filled to capacity and many workers were sleeping at the time of the crash. Gretl and I were asleep in our apartment. They aroused us and all the personnel living around the area. Along with other nurses and doctors, we were rushed to the scene of the accident in old beat up Army trucks.

On the way the head nurses handed out bandage material and other supplies for first aid. Trucks and ambulances from other hospitals were arriving on the scene when we got there.

The darkness made it hard to see how bad the situation was until they brought some emergency lights. Many of the injured were moaning and crying. Some had to be cut from under twisted steel. One man's head was sticking out from under a metal piece that had pinned his entire body down. He was still alive! Broken glass caused many serious wounds. I worked on one person, then another, searching with my first aid kit hanging around my shoulders. I left the dead behind and tried to help where it was needed. Those we could move we carried to the trucks. The one from our hospital filled quickly. One doctor drove back with them to the hospital where nurses were getting the operating table ready. It was almost dawn when we returned to the hospital to help with patients that were still in need of care and a bed.

Not until morning were we able to change our bloodstained clothing, take a shower, and get a few hours of sleep. We had worked to exhaustion but by midmorning things were under control and all those who had gotten hurt were taken care of.

The Railroad Minister from East Germany came early the next day to visit the accident victims. He brought flowers, candy, and champagne. He went to great lengths apologizing and expressing the hope that they would recover soon. After thanking the personnel who had worked all night, he went on to other hospitals where other injured people were being cared for.

After a few weeks some of the injured were able to go home. Some still needed care, which they would get in their hometowns. The satisfaction of helping, and seeing the results of healing, lifted my spirits and life again seemed worthwhile.

To fill my lonely hours on free days, I often visited Father Hofmann. I was always hopeful for some news about Volker. Father Hofmann wanted to visit Volker in the penitentiary in Bautzen where he thought Volker was held. They told him, "No visits, no gifts." He said he only wanted to leave a small pound cake for Volker at the jail but that the guards had taken the cake and smashed it, as if they thought there was something hidden in it. Father Hoffman became very depressed because he did not get to see Volker. Even though he was glad to see me, our visits were very sad.

Carrying food obtained from my Wismut ration cards and little gifts for everyone, I took Father Hoffman home with me for part of my Christmas holiday. Members of the family called him Uncle Hofmann, which seemed to please him. He responded to every question with long detailed answers. He was well read and educated; it was a pleasure to have him around. Best of all for me was the news that Volker's sentence was reduced from 15 to 8 years. But eight years still seemed like a lifetime to me. Mama's home was now directly across the street from the church and a small park about two blocks large surrounded the church. When she looked out of the window she could see senior citizens walking and sitting on benches in the summer. The house was warm and the snow made our Christmas beautiful. Ortwin and Hartmut were entertaining their girlfriends for the holidays but there was still enough food for everyone. No Christmas *stollen*, but a cake just the same.

As we attended the Christmas service, I thought of Volker and our Christmas the year before. The past year had brought so much happiness, and yet even greater sorrow. I cried silently. I felt so empty as Father Hoffman and I traveled back to work.

January of 1953 brought a severe flu epidemic. Many seriously ill people died a short time after being admitted to the hospital. One night, I was on special duty with patients needing shots every hour to keep their hearts pounding. I stood by the bed of one patient and held his blue hand as he gasped for air.

"You have survived the night," I said. "It is morning it will be easier now."

He held my hand and nodded, then fell back and died. I could not hold back the tears. That morning, five patients passed away. People were being admitted in such advanced stages of illness that medical care was ineffective. Those few patients we were able to nurse through the epidemic were our only reward for many of those sleepless nights.

A severe winter left the hospital grounds in need of much cleanup and repair. Since all the custodians were now big Party VIPs, who did the custodial work? The nurses! The doctors were also asked to do their share, but they flatly refused. The Party bosses fumed but that was all.

In February I joined other nurses in sweeping snow off the sidewalks. The flu epidemic had subsided and we were back to our regular nursing activities. Our free time was used to work on the hospital grounds, clean around shrubs, and to do general outside work. When I watched the way some of the nurses handled a broom, I had to laugh, which resulted in very little work being done.

This continued for a while until another event came to change the course of my life.

It happened quickly. Our hospital was ordered by the Russians to become a tuberculosis sanatorium. All patients in our hospital were transferred to the new and larger Erlabrunn Hospital.

Tuberculosis patients came, spitting into little cups they carried around with them. The first patients were ambulatory, followed by those with more advanced stages of the disease.

All nurses under 25 years of age were told to look for another place to work since we could more easily contract TB. The prospect of more rest and better food seemed to outweigh the risks to Gretl, she stayed. So did other nurses I had become good friends with. As specialists on tuberculosis came, our doctors left.

I sent resumes to the hospitals in Chemnitz and Potsdam, both near Berlin, and received prompt answers from both. I could start immediately in either hospital. I rushed home and begged Mama to approve of my going to Potsdam City Hospital.

"Mama, I cannot stand the Communist ways anymore. One of these days they're going to get me too, just like they got Volker. I've seen the West and I want to go there and work."

Potsdam was still East Germany but was also a gateway to the West.

Mama and Christine cried.

"Mama, as much as I want to live near you and the family, the Communist ways never made any sense to me. I don't believe they want us to live better, ever. All they do is promise us things. For years only promises and Party doctrine. I am tired of it. I hate it."

"But Irene, you have always loved Chemnitz. Here you would be with all the family."

"I am sick to death of this political indoctrination. Every week we have to listen to more political speeches. See what they have done to Volker? I want to be free of all this!"

As I spoke I realized how strong my desire for freedom had become. My brothers had their own interests in Chemnitz, including plans to marry. Since they did not know how life could be in the West, their longings for freedom were not as strong as mine, for they loved that old town Chemnitz too much.

We all shed tears when I left for Potsdam. Ortwin clung to me as if he knew we would never see each other again.

FLIGHT- 1953

In Potsdam, a city of about 136,000 inhabitants, I rented a furnished room in the Weinbergstrasse, which was only walking distance from Sanssouci Castle and Gardens. The Sanssouci Castle was built by Knobelsdorff according to plans by Friedrich II from 1745 to 1747.

The Park of Sanssouci's area is about three square kilometers. It had its beginning in 1744 and was enlarged by Garden Director P.J. Lenne under the reign of Friedrich Whilhelm III and Friedrich Wilhelm IV. It has marvelous parks with carpet-like beds, borders, circular flowerbeds and fountains decorated with sculptures.

It also was eight blocks from the hospital. My windows faced toward a small front yard, and then the street as was customary in the old Potsdam area.

I liked my landlady and we often sat in her kitchen and talked. I trusted her and we became good friends.

Across the hall lived an old informer from Nazi days. Now she did the same thing for the Communist Party. Frau Loose was so curious she would burst into the hall whenever she heard the slightest movement in the building. Sometimes I turned my key very slowly to avoid alerting this overzealous woman of my presence. I seldom succeeded.

I worked eight-hour shifts at the hospital, six days a week. When I reported for work the first day, the nurse major looked at me for a full minute, then said, "We are happy to hire you but we hope you did not come here only to run to the West."

After being introduced to all the wards, they assigned me to surgery. Potsdam Hospital was much larger than both the Wiesen and Rabenstein hospitals put together. It took me a while to learn how to get around in that large building complex.

My free afternoons were spent in the famous Sanssouci Castle and Gardens. At the time I was there, the Castle was getting restored to its original glamour and tourists were rare. In the future, I knew, I wouldn't be able to sit there in private with my books. Things would change and too many people would invade the gardens, the orangery and all my secret places.

As I walked to and from work, I passed the Russian's command post close to the gate of the castle gardens. Their loud march music drummed in people's ears, day and night. After dark their building blazed with lights, spot-lighting the big red star high on the roof. In front a large red flag was displayed. The whole building reminded me of the Commandantura in Riesa, where Krista and I were in a wet prison cell. When I passed that building I wondered how many prisoners were now held there. Most people I knew avoided coming anywhere near there.

I lived near the best of Germany's past, the castle and gardens, and the worst of her present, the Communist rule that lay like a choking mantle over our country.

Shortly after I started my work in Potsdam, Hartmut got married, but I was not given leave to go home for his wedding. Ortwin's wedding soon followed. On a long weekend I was able to buy him a pair of shoes that Ortwin needed so badly. Thus, I headed home carrying a small suitcase and a sack of potatoes, which was more welcome than flowers. Carrying all these things on the train was nothing unusual since there were still many people who traveled into the country in the hope of finding food to stretch their meager food rations. Before returning to Potsdam, we talked about where Ortwin and his bride would live.

"It's going to be a while before we can have our own place. Until then we will live with Herta's mother because she has more room for us than Mama. They are beginning to build apartments soon and we will register for one next week. It might take five to eight years but we must be on the list. We also must help with the construction in our spare time."

Since there was a shortage of men to work in construction, every family who wanted a new apartment had to put in thousands of working hours after working a job in the day. In the evening they labored as construction workers with the hope that they would one day move into one of those apartments. For this backbreaking work there was no pay. Only credit for each hour they worked. There were no extra food rations for this either.

As I traveled back to Potsdam I longed to see Volker. I wondered if we would ever have the chance to live in an apartment as Ortwin and Herta were hoping to do. All my letters I wrote to the jail came back. He was not allowed to receive mail. I knew he must feel terrible and I prayed for him that he would be strong enough to endure his unfair punishment.

While walking to work one day, I saw a guard standing in front of a photo studio and a policeman posting a sign saying, *ZUTRITT VERBOTEN* (OFF LIMITS). My landlady explained in a hushed voice that the owner had been arrested. But the police spread the rumor that the owner had escaped to the West, leaving all his expensive equipment behind. A few days later the same thing happened at several other stores. One day they are open for business, the next day the store was guarded by police. People were disappearing.

One of the apartment buildings was converted into a prison and Russian soldiers, together with German guards, put up barbed wire around the building. In many windows the glass was broken and iron bars were put on them. I grieved for every poor soul that was imprisoned in there. Of course I heard many rumors, especially when I stood in line for a few soup bones from the butchery located near the prison building. If it was true, what they were saying, I felt a chill through my bones.

I wrote to Mama, urging her to come with Claus and Christine. Her answer convinced me she would never leave Chemnitz.

"An old woman is like an old tree. You cannot transplant it. Now that the boys have married I am busy helping them. Hartmut has a job on the government farm and lives in an old beat up house, you ought to see it. But they make it livable. Their first child is on the way. I will be a grandmother soon. Ortwin has a job in the city."

Holding the letter that told me no matter what they had to go through, they loved their homeland and they would stay no matter what was happening, I felt very lonely. I knew there were people who felt this way about their birthplace. But I never thought my family would be among them.

Most of our patients in Wiesen Hospital were young miners. Here in Potsdam people of all ages came to be treated and I became acquainted with the more serious diseases of cancer, diabetes, and many other serious ailments. Many patients with cancer of the colon came to our ward. Although they survived the operation, not enough had been done for them to survive for too long afterward. The treatment was not as modern as it is today.

A three month old boy with leukemia was brought to our ward. Everybody just loved him. He needed many blood transfusions and after each time he would revive and be quite lively, only to become listless again in a few days. He would lie as though he were dead. He had type B blood, the same as mine. I volunteered to give blood. I was so happy for him, to be revived with my blood. But each day he would lapse further toward death and in spite of a series of treatments, he passed away. The doctors did not know what to do other than give him transfusions and study his blood.

We had our humorous experiences too. One of our smaller wards was occupied by a Party member who had lost one of her eyes. It had been replaced with a glass one. One day I washed her glass eye and set it in wrong.

When the doctor made his rounds, her glass eye was looking in a different direction while the other eye looked at him. It looked so weird that instead of helping her, the nurses laughed like crazy. Of course they did not tell her what I had done. Later, after everyone had left, I corrected my mistake. This was a very commanding person and she always tried to get people in trouble, so we played little tricks on her.

One night I wheeled a deceased patient to the morgue in the basement of the hospital. Bodies of all ages lay next to each other on different long wooden tables, covered with stainless steel sheeting. Some of them were covered completely, others had their upper bodies uncovered. Their names and information about their deaths was written on little cards fastened to their big toes.

"They use some of these bodies to make autopsies when teaching," explained a nurse. She chuckled, then continued, "Once they picked up several bodies. One was a woman with an unborn child. When they sewed her up again they were in such a hurry, they forgot to put the infant in her. When they finished with the next, a male body, they stuffed the little one in his belly just to get rid of it. Who would know or care?" She sighed.

I shuddered and left, glad to be healthy and alive. I surely did not want to die here!

In our hospital a Party official was assigned to each ward. They found this the best way to control everyone in such a large building complex. One afternoon, just prior to our weekly political lecture, I excused myself to go to the restroom. Our Political Officer, a male nurse, followed me into the ladies room and waited for me outside the toilet booth.

"Of all the nerve---why do you come in here?" I asked very angry and in disgust.

"We have nurses that jump out of the window to avoid coming to the meeting," he replied with a sneer.

"Through a third floor window?" I laughed sarcastically.

"Yes. They jump to that balcony."

"I see," I replied walking over to the window. "That makes good sense."

Angrily, I pushed him aside as I left the room, saying, "Maybe I'll try it some time."

The food allowance in Potsdam was much less than I had received in Wiesen. Ration cards ranged from A, the most, to E, the least. Mine was a D card. I could only afford 300 grams of meat in one *decade* (ten days) and I often stood in line for a full hour at the butchery only to see the meat bone supply run out before my turn came. I was never able to buy meat itself, only bones with some meat on them. My total rations would never be enough to even buy a steak. I ate my main meal in the hospital dining room each day in exchange for some of my ration coupons and money. Those meals were always meatless, usually sauerkraut and peeled potatoes or grits cooked in milk.

In this hospital dining room I became friends with Lottie Buchner, a nurse with five years experience. She was a pretty girl, about my age, and just a little shorter in height then I. She was always full of energy. Her boyfriend worked for a newspaper. One day she came by my home and wanted me to meet her attractive, curly-haired, tall fiancée. They were a nice, interesting couple and I liked them both.

After I served tea and we talked briefly, he asked, "How would you like to work for the Americans?"

Amazed that they trusted me enough to reveal their political activities in such an open way, I asked, "What in the world could they want to know?"

"I am sure you have all kinds of information from the uranium mines. They will contact you."

"This is silly. I think this is a trap."

"No trap," he said. "They will tell you what they want to know and you will be well paid."

I thought of Volker. I certainly did not want to risk being sent to a labor camp, nor had I forgotten my back-breaking experience in the uranium mines.

"We felt you could be trusted. Think about it," said Lottie, "but say nothing to anyone."

"You can be sure of that. With my luck, I would only get in trouble with the Party people. It so happens we have one informer right across the hall."

"We are trying to save enough money to get married," he said.

"I hope on the Western side. I cannot picture you two living here the rest of your lives. I admire your courage."

When they left I was still uncommitted to such a dangerous mission. For now I needed time to make my own plans.

When exploration of the Sanssouci castle and gardens, which were just in walking distance, ceased to hold my interest, I began riding the electric U-Bahn. Although controlled entirely by East Germany, the U-Bahn traveled from Potsdam, through West Berlin, and into East Berlin again. Each time I rode the U-Bahn I watched and I learned.

Many people got off the U-Bahn in West Berlin. At all train stops on the East side, people were spot checked by armed Russian border guards. We always held our IDs high so they could read them quickly. Without a proper ID, one could not get through the barrier at the station. We had to show where we lived and worked and give a reasonable explanation for our travel.

After Russian guards separated out suspected persons for further checking, the German police mustered them into a large room that served as a police station. People caught in a search raid had to put their purchases on a long table and handbags were searched. They ran their hands over the body on the outside of the clothes to determine if things might be concealed.

Persons in possession of forbidden Western items were transferred to another police station in the city. Each case was punished according to the degree of the offense. Even foodstuff and soaps were forbidden. We had such bad soap powder that it could only be called sand. Western soaps of any kind were welcomed articles for the black market.

Confiscated items were sold in a store run by the government in Potsdam. I and others often crowded in front of those store windows to see dream items such as shoes, ski boots, ladies' lace negligees, sheer colorful gowns, dresses, coats and cameras. All items were of high quality and prices were even higher. Few people could afford them. The exchange rate was still five East Mark to one West Mark and four West Mark to one American Dollar. That gives one an idea of how little East German marks were worth. Next to nothing.

Persons caught trying to escape from East Germany were usually sentenced for ten to twenty years at hard labor. I knew the prisons were full because buildings other than the regular prison were now being used to hold the prisoners. I could see the barbed wire strung over windows of these makeshift prisons and guards were often seen standing in front of buildings that looked deserted. Yet in spite of the danger, many people were escaping to the West.

The West Berlin radio station, RIAS, followed each news broadcast with the warning "If you escape into West Berlin, go immediately to Kuno Fischer Strasse. Do not talk to anyone but a West Berlin Policeman. Trust nobody."

RIAS broadcasted a program on Saturday nights called "The Islanders," an appropriate title since West Berlin was an island in East Germany. I liked the way they made fun of the East Berlin way of life because it always was true. People flocked to the radios to hear RIAS, although it was officially forbidden. Sometimes, the old man Adenauer would speak. In a fatherly voice he said, "We are all Germans, we are one people." He made us feel as if he had compassion for our situation and that he would like to help if he only could.

A letter came from Gretl. As I opened it the East German radio broadcasted their daily warnings again of the penalties if caught going into West Berlin. The only exception was if one was lucky enough to have a job in the West, but people who worked in the West and lived in the East got harassed by getting searched on border crossings. Trains were often stopped so they usually came to work late. Then in the evenings at rush hour, people again had a hard time coming back home since the trains would not run at all hours. This was nothing but harassment but people had no other means of transportation at the time. They just had to live with the nuisance. Many scuffles occurred and many tears were shed, and not just by women. The East German authorities hoped that by harassing people like that, they would give up their jobs in the West and start working in East Germany where they lived. Every time I heard those threats on the radio I turned it off in disgust.

I sat down to read Gretl's letter. Another letter was enclosed and addressed to her boyfriend, Ottokar Mangold, in West Berlin. He had escaped and wanted her to come to him. She was afraid to risk it.

Gretl wanted me to hand-deliver the letter to him at one of the refugee camps. In spite of the danger I decided to try.

On my next free day I placed the letter in a hidden pocket fastened inside my skirt. I bought a ticket from Potsdam to Henningsdorf. Such a ticket was easy to obtain since Henningsdorf was opposite from Potsdam and still in East Germany, but one had to pass through West Berlin. This way, I gave the impression that I would take a ride through West Berlin without stepping off the train in the West. When I got on the train again coming back, nobody would even know where I had been. My ID would verify where I lived and worked and on my way to see Ottokar, I was careful to appear unconcerned by reading an East German newspaper. As I rode the U-Bahn, I watched those who got on and off at each station. I looked for police and guards. The closer I came to my stop, the more tense I became.

The train slowed for the stop. I folded my newspaper, placed it on the seat and rose to leave. I stepped off the train and walked briskly toward the steps that led up to the street. As I reached the street, a great flood of relief filled my body. I had made it! I was safe!

I located the refugee camp in a huge building that was evidently a converted factory. The whole area was surrounded by a six-foot high chain-linked fence. Large trash cans full of garbage were stacked behind the gate.

At the entrance I showed my passport, my ID from the hospital, and a passport photo. After recording my ID information they sent me to another office where they recorded the information again. Then they called Ottokar over the loudspeaker. In a short time he came, almost running. He thought his papers had come through with his clearance to leave Berlin and go into West Germany.

"Irene!" he called in surprise, "How happy I am to see you."

He told the officials he was willing to talk to me, then said, "They are always on guard against infiltrators and people often get kidnapped."

Taking both my hands in his, he seemed excited and on the verge of tears. "This waiting to get processed gets to you."

We walked into the yard and sat on an empty box. As we talked, Ottokar turned his head a couple of times to hide his tears. I gave him Gretl's letter. As he read it, he kept shaking his head, "Why? Oh, why is she so frightened? She could be here with me right now. You could help her get across to the West, couldn't you?"

"Yes I could," I assured him.

It was plain to see he was disheartened by the letter. I gave him a chance to change the subject by asking, "How are you managing? There must be many people here."

"This camp is crowded, as you can see. We are all waiting for our papers to be processed. A few leave every week to go into West Germany. Those that have been discovered as spies are sent back to East Germany. Although this is a temporary shelter, it is well organized. Hundreds of thousands have already come this year and they just keep pouring in. The authorities don't know where to put them all but they let them come anyway."

I explained to him how lucky those people are now that West Germany is accepting people from East Germany. "Yes, no one wants to live under the Russians. My family is not happy there either but when it was easier to cross the border some years ago, the West did not accept people from the Russian Zone. They would have sent us back and then we would have all landed in jail or in a deathcamp built by the NKVD called "*Internierungslager.*" It was like the one *Fuenfeichen* and others. There Stalin committed mass murder on German soil and after the war, thousands of Germans of all kinds. Those mass graves were discovered after the Berlin Wall came down.

"Some families are lucky enough to have escaped together, although too many have left loved ones behind. I am one of those," Ottokar sobbed.

I put my hand on his shoulder trying to comfort him. "I left everything I owned," he said. "And I will have to start from the bottom. But I know I can make it, Irene. Gretl could too. I love her and she wants me to forget her and start a new life without her." Tears poured down his face and he held my hand tightly.

"I'm so sorry, Ottokar. It's the same with Mama. She is so intimidated by radio broadcasts and informers everywhere that she too is afraid to leave."

"Once I get cleared, I hope to go to Canada and start a nutria farm." Saying this he looked more hopeful.

"What about your acting career?" I asked.

"I will first make enough money from acting to buy a nutria farm." He laughed.

Dreams, I thought. *Everyone must have dreams*. "How is it with the other refugees?" I asked.

"I don't know anyone and it's better that way. From the moment I walked into Kuno Fischer Strasse it was absolute silence to everyone. Those big signs posted around the walls high above our heads did it. They read:

PST, DO NOT SPEAK
DO NOT TELL, ANYONE BUT AUTHORITIES YOUR
NAME
DO NOT TRUST ANYONE

There must have been a thousand people standing inside the small courtyard. Not a word was spoken, not even a sound from the children.

"It isn't even safe here in West Berlin?" I was aghast.

106

"One man who talked, told me he saw someone kidnapped off the street. A man was pulled into a car and they drove off. He figured it was someone East Germany wanted back."

"But how could they?" I asked.

"Think about it, Irene. The West has no border guards. They are all in the East. The Police State begins when you enter East Berlin. They are kidnapping people regularly."

"You will never regret leaving, Ottokar, but the price of freedom is high."

"I try to look on the bright side, Irene. Remembering your courage, I'll make it. I have to."

The ease with which I had gotten into West Berlin and out once more quickened my interest in trying it again. I learned that nurses who worked with me in the hospital also went many times into West Berlin. They gathered their antiques and went into the West to sell them. When they came back the nurses and doctors showed off their nylons, pretty shoes, and fancy underwear and other items.

The Charlottenburg Youth Center in West Berlin became my favorite haunt. Youth from both East and West met there to enjoy games and reading material. Occasionally they took us to a movie theater. Although I felt conspicuous walking in the streets three abreast with a large group of teenagers, my desire to see a western movie was stronger than any embarrassment I felt. The free meal served late in the afternoon was also an attraction for me. People trying to escape into West Berlin without maps and no understanding of police procedures usually stumbled into a well organized net. Many were shot and killed. The seriously injured were brought to our hospital for treatment.

A young boy from Leipzig, a couple from Frankenberg, two teenage boys from Dresden, and an 18-year old girl from Halle all lay in isolation rooms under 24-hour guard. No one was allowed near them except doctors and occasionally a nurse. Nurses and doctors had to sign in and out to treat the wounded.

One day Doctor R_____ walked into the nurses' duty room and said, "That dumb kid, why didn't he get more information before he tried to escape. Those kids never think of the consequences if they're caught. I feel so sorry for him. Have you seen any of them, Schwester Irene?"

"I saw the couple from Frankenberg. Their heavy Erzgebirge dialect puts them under suspicion the minute they open their mouths. I think they have a brother living in West Germany who is waiting for them. They thought it would be so easy to go through Berlin, but they arrived at night and missed the last U-Bahn. Since they had no idea where to cross, they found a room for the night in a small hotel. After they registered, the hotel owner reported them to the police. Before they were ready for bed the police were there knocking on their door. When they tried to jump out of the window they were shot at. They have been interrogated and were apparently caught in a lie. They were huddled together in their room like two frightened rabbits. It's heartbreaking, Doctor R_____"

Shaking his head, the doctor left the room.

A group of young boys tried to escape by running along the Babelsberg Bridge. They swung themselves up to catch the U-Bahn and must have panicked when they saw Russian guards with their machine guns at the ticket entrance. They thought they could cross the bridge and get back on the train. Some of them were caught without being shot; others must have gotten on the train. When the guards saw them running they stopped the train. While the guards were checking IDs one young boy jumped off the train and ran. They shot him. Two bullets were removed, one from his shoulder blade and one from his kidney area. He said there were others arrested with him who were not part of his group. It was just their misfortune to be on that train at that time. Had they been on another train they probably would have made it.

He was just a baby, trying to escape to freedom. When the other nurses and I saw what they had done to this boy, we felt very sad. Doctor R_____ was doing his best to keep the boy in the hospital as long as possible. Guards, stationed outside the hospital rooms constantly reminded us "to give prisoners necessities only." When prisoners were able to travel they were taken to a prison hospital.

***

I sat in the Sanssouci Gardens reading a letter from Mama. *The propaganda machine must be pounding louder in Chemnitz than in East Berlin,* I thought. She wanted to see me but was afraid to come near Berlin.

"...People are constantly warned to expect 25 years of hard labor if caught trying to escape. Ortwin's brother-in-law, only 17 years old, was caught at the East-West border and is now in Bautzen Prison."

It wasn't fair, a 17-year old sentenced to 25 years of hard labor; I had heard that this happened in Russia, but now it was happening in Germany too? Her letter continued.

"Now that Stalin is dead, it must get better. The Russians produced Tschaikowsky and Tolstoy and their dancers are world famous. We'll just have to make the best of it and live with them."

Mama was frightened. I wanted to go home, to see everyone again. I knew they were finding it hard to accept the idea of my working in Potsdam.

ARRESTED

I visited the Charlottenburg Youth Center and read about Stalin's death. It was as if the world celebrated this terrible man's death. I was amazed to read that some Russians actually cried when Stalin died. My landlady commented, "Even the devil has followers."

I now spent my free time in the West Berlin Youth Center, reading books and magazines, along with all the literature forbidden in East Germany.

"Could I borrow some of these? I'll bring them back." They smiled and said, "Of course, but be careful. Don't get caught with them."

I was about to leave when someone announced that an American movie was going to be shown. I just could not pass it up. They put a group of people, mostly East Berliners, together and we left immediately for the movie theater. Some of this movie is still in my mind; it was the first time that I realized how people from the USA had also suffered because of the war. The title was: "The Five Sullivans." When we left the movie theater, most people were wiping their eyes.

After the show I boarded the U-Bahn for Potsdam. It was pitch dark and when the train rode through East Berlin, and I was already dreading the walk from the station home. Since the streetlights were so far apart, women often got molested in the dark spots.

The train was filled to capacity. As I gave my ticket to the German employee, I noticed that because of the large crowd, the Russian Guards were holding about 20 people, and then letting a hundred go by before separating out the next 20 or so. This time I was stopped. I had never been searched before. Suddenly I remembered the Western literature. Ice cold fear gripped my body. There was no place to discard my borrowed material.

We were all ushered into the interrogation room at the Potsdam U-Bahn Station. The woman ahead of me was carrying a bag full of eggs. Although the woman was crying and pleading, the Russian took them out of her hands. After writing down what he had taken, he picked up the eggs to take them away. She became very angry and, in great desperation, grabbed the bag. He had not expected this and resisted only partly. She ripped the bag open and started screaming. Then she quickly threw the eggs down to the floor and trampled on them. She cursed in German. He cursed in Russian. The rest of the people cheered for a minute but were commanded to keep quiet. It was a big mess. In the scuffle, I threw my magazines on the floor hoping no one would see where they came from.

Too many police and Russians were watching. Everyone saw me! I was signaled to move away from the rest of the people. It was amazing how many people they arrested for having such little things as soap, food, or small amounts of Western money in their possession.

I was immediately labeled a dangerous spy, as the papers were considered propaganda material from the West. They treated me as if I was their enemy. I was held at the police station all that night. Early

112

the next morning, I complained of extreme pain in my stomach and said that I had been pushed when they arrested me.

After they made several phone calls, they took me to the Potsdam City Hospital where I worked. This was just what I had hoped for. Perhaps someone here would be able to help me.

Under guard I was taken to an examining room. I knew the guard was standing outside my door and no one would be allowed to come near except by permission of the police. My watch and other valuables had been taken away but I knew it was almost noon when Doctor R_____ came in to check out my stomach complaint.

Obviously, rumors that a nurse from this hospital had been arrested had spread like wildfire.

"Schwester Irene! What have you done, you foolish kid?" he whispered. "You of all people should have known how careful you must be."

"I know. I've made a serious stupid mistake." I explained to him why I was arrested. "Have you heard what they have decided?"

"An emergency conference has been called and people you work with are being questioned."

"About what, Doctor R_____?"

"The usual. Are you attending regular political lectures? What you said? Who you talked with? How many trips you made to West Berlin? Why this, why that? I can tell you, they are not interested to know if you are a good or bad nurse. They only want to know how you think politically. That is all that is important to them."

I covered my face with my hands and the weight of the world a came crashing down on my emotions. Doctor R_____ took my

113

hands away from my face and looked squarely at me. "I can tell you that those who know you in the administration office are insisting that you are not as bad as the Party people are trying to make you appear. But you know how vengeful Party people can be and they usually have the last word."

He walked toward the door, then turned and said, "They said they are contacting Wiesen. They want any file Wiesen has on you. As you know, everyone has a file and it stays with you until death. I'll come back if I can get in. The excuse will be to see how the medication is working."

He left and I waited. I knew when they learned about my work in the uranium mines they would find my present acts serious enough for a long jail sentence, probably 25 years. *My life is over*, I thought.

The hours ticked away. Then the key turned and I heard Doctor R_____'s voice. I waited tensely as he entered the room.

"Well, you foolish girl, how could you do such a dumb thing?" He put his hand on my shoulder and continued. "Things look very bad, Irene. You will get a long prison sentence at least. You know as well as I do the labor camps always have space for people making mistakes."

I felt the blood drain from my face and I trembled. He looked concerned, but I knew he was angry. He looked at me and his eyes narrowed in thought.

"There is only one thing you can do, Irene. Get out that window and run as fast as you can. I will stall them as long as possible. Pick up your birth certificate and other important papers. No, wait. I don't know if you have enough time. Go straight to the U-Bahn and into

West Berlin. Here are two marks for a ticket. The guard will see that you are in bed when I go out. Let him lock the door, then run!"

He unlocked the window with the master key and leaned it together again. The window had two wings that opened inward.

"Dress and get into bed. I can only wait a minute. Hurry!"

Quickly, I put my clothes on, even my shoes. He kissed my cheek and whispered, "I'll stall them as long as I can. May God be with you. Hurry!"

He knocked on the door, indicating to the guard that he was finished with me. Seeing that I was in bed, the guard locked the door after Doctor R_____ went out.

I threw the covers off and ran to the window. I pulled it open, sat on the sill, and swung my legs out, then jumped about two yards down from a first floor window. I stumbled briefly from the drop, but quickly ran. I was gasping for air when I reached home.

In my panic I pulled drawers out onto the floor while looking for my birth certificate. I grabbed my only good dress, some other small items, and a few eating utensils. The thought flashed through my mind that Ottokar said eating utensils are important to have. I packed underwear and other things I don't even remember. I was too nervous to search for anything I might need for the coming weeks. Listening for a knock on the door, my breathing sounded very loud and the tension made my neck muscles cramp. I was not thinking rationally. I changed into my nursing uniform thinking maybe that would help me get by the guards.

I stuffed things into a small suitcase and snapped the lid shut. Why hadn't I planned this better? I could have mailed some of my things to Mama and had her send them to me later. I was sure I had taken too much time. As I opened the door, I dropped my suitcase. The informer heard me trying to lock my door and came out of her apartment like a pistol shot. She saw my suitcase but I didn't wait for her questions.

"I have a couple of days off and want to spend them with my mother," I said. "I have to hurry to catch the train."

She smiled slyly and I knew that is what she would report. I ran down the street, three blocks to the next street car stop. Once inside, I thought everyone in the coach must be looking at me and know where I was headed. My head throbbed. I felt sick.

If I need to, I thought, *I'll leave my suitcase in the streetcar and run*. I thought of the young boy shot twice and still in the hospital under guard. Yesterday, I would never have dreamed that today I would be the one being hunted.

I stepped down from the streetcar and walked across the road from the Potsdam U-Bahn station. Suddenly I stopped, frozen with fear. So many police--they were swarming around much more than usual. I was sure they were waiting just for me. They must have already been to my home. This was not the place to board the U-Bahn.

Turning my back, I moved quickly to conceal myself in the crowd and wait for another streetcar. Within minutes I boarded a car for Babelsberg, further into Berlin. I never thought this kind of situation would arise. I always thought there would be plenty of time. Why didn't I have a better plan? Now I felt like a frightened rabbit darting about in utter panic.

There were fewer police at the Babelsberg stop. I left the streetcar, entered the U-Bahn station and bought a ticket with a return since the U-Bahn enters West Berlin nearby. A return ticket was above suspicion. As I walked up to the barrier, a Russian soldier with the usual machine gun and an East German policeman were checking tickets and people were holding their IDs up.

They let me go through, even with my suitcase. I sensed that my nursing uniform was helping me get by. They had even smiled. Two very young guards stood by with dangerous guns in their hands, ready to shoot on command. If someone died they would say, "I only did my duty." Had they been older, they would have been more experienced and more suspicious. They would not have smiled.

I walked along the platform, trying to stay behind a pillar, and acting as though I was reading the train schedule.

The U-Bahn arrived. I got on, still not sure if I could make it. If they thought I was on this train, they could always stop it. Even now someone could be inside searching for me. A family sat across from me in the coach, a husband, wife, and two children. They were well dressed and must have been "somebody" in East Germany.

The husband was drinking heavily. He stood up and asked silly questions of everyone. His wife sat there crying and the children seemed just as frightened as I was. He shouted out loud, "Life is only bearable by being drunk." Other people looked embarrassed and tried not to answer him. He did not listen to his wife and finally she gave up. Everyone sensed that this family was about to escape. I was very frightened and I was sure that this fool would get us all into trouble.

117

He looked at me and asked me what I thought of him. When I could not ignore him any longer I said, much too loudly, "*Setzen Sie sich*" (sit down). I surprised even myself by the tone of my voice. He was aghast for a moment and actually sat down quietly until a few minutes later when he started all over again.

Dear God, let me leave this place safely.

As I saw the Charlottenburg sign the U-Bahn slowed. I walked off the train and down the platform to the steps, still carrying my suitcase. No policemen were in sight. I walked up a few steps and onto a sunny street.

The impact of it all suddenly engulfed me. Trembling, I put my suitcase down and sat on it. There on the sidewalk of West Berlin I wept uncontrollably. My body jerked with sobs and the tears washed down my face, wetting my hands and dress. People rushed by me and no one stopped. Finally, when the stream of tears ceased, a great emptiness came over me. Less than an hour before only tension and fear had gripped my body.

Why should anyone stop? They probably saw this scene every day at this same place. I was about to pick up my little suitcase in one hand and was drying my eyes with the other, when a policeman saw me and walked towards me.

"Now, now. Things will get better," he promised in a soothing voice. This only made me break out in tears again. He picked up my suitcase and carried it almost up to Kuno Fischer Strasse. I thanked him and he warned me not to speak to anyone but the authorities.

"There are many agents from the East around here and kidnapping is an everyday event. If they want you back in East

Germany, they will come over here and get you. Please be careful. Above all, do not give your name or where you come from to anyone but an official." He handed me my suitcase. "They'll take care of you in there. Expect to wait in long lines but be patient. Today you are free."

On that warm day in May of 1953, I began the long and tedious task of being processed through the refugee camp. Unprepared for the human flood that reached for freedom rather than live under Russia's oppressive hand, West Germany and the allied governments struggled mightily to sort out and care for the millions who came seeking freedom.

Two months later, after establishing an address, I received my first letter from Mama. Anxiously, I read:

July 1953

Dearest Irene,

Thank God you are safe. I have much to tell you about the police search. The day after you left Potsdam a noisy motorcade pulled up in front of our building here in Chemnitz. Everyone was so excited they ran out of the building or stuck their heads out of the windows. Others who were hiding could only worry what it was all about. They all wanted to see what was going on and hoped it would be the other guy who would be arrested. As you know, that is always the case. I looked out of the window and saw two cars, one civilian and one police, led by four motorcycles. They all had grim faces and were, of course, in uniform.

It never occurred to me that they were coming to see us. I saw one of the girls from downstairs go across the street and into the church. I thought she was trying to get away from the police. I knew the police saw her, but they came into our building instead. Imagine my shock when they rang our doorbell and pounded on the door.

I was so frightened. I didn't know what had happened. They were so sure you were here they burst into the apartment and looked through all the rooms and closets. Some ran up the staircase probably looking at the roof. Then they asked for you. They must have thought you were a dangerous spy or something. When they said "Irene" I knew I must stall for time. I was not sure if you were safe in West Berlin or exactly where you were.

I said I didn't know where you were but that you had left the house. Then I thought of the girl crossing the street and said, "You must have seen her." I couldn't imagine why they sent two cars and four police on motorcycles to arrest just one person, but they must have had their orders from Berlin and that meant high priority. After they questioned me in a very unfriendly way, I told them you might have left to go to Euba to visit some friends.

They also asked all the neighbors if they had seen you. I learned later that they had searched the main road all the way to Euba. They even found Krista's family. Someone must have told them you and Krista were friends. You know how her brothers like to trick the police. They said you must be coming through the fields and that you never took the main road. They ran their motorcycles right through the plowed fields at the government farm looking for you. I am sure they did not like to see that, their motorcycles were full of mud but they sure went through a lot of trouble trying to find you. They searched for hours. Krista said they heard the motorcycle noise for the longest time even in the dark. When they returned to Chemnitz, they were very irritated and exhausted.

They were angry and warned me that when you came home, day or night, I must report you to the police or face arrest myself. Apparently many people in the neighborhood were alerted to keep an eye out for you and report anything to the police. The police watched this building for days. So you see my dear, they really did not know where you were.

The first letter I received was not intercepted but they seized the second one. They knew then that you had escaped. Still, they could not get any definite information on where you were in the refugee camps and the search was called off.

I hope you get this letter before you move again. I know you would not have left unless it was absolutely necessary.

Take care of yourself, Irene, and remember we all love you very much.

Mama

As I put the letter aside I closed my eyes and thanked God for my freedom from the unbearable restriction of Communism. I thought of Volker. If he survived the eight years in Bautzen, I would hear from him through Mama. Mama was where she had to be and I had to learn to accept that. Thousands of families were kept apart because of the division of the country. I was not alone.

At age 23 I could now live my life with the freedom I had wanted for so long.

I was one of 331,000 people who escaped to freedom in West Berlin in 1953.

EPILOGUE

For years after the war, there was so much chaos in Germany. Small towns that were not bombed sometimes owned a castle or fortress with large rooms. They were used for quarters for homeless and jobless people. The West German government did a tremendous job, over just a few years, to create housing and find work for all those people. After all that was set up, they has to make room again for thousands of German prisoners of war that came home from the USA and some trains full of POW's from Russia.

I saw trains rolling into the railroad stations with POW's wearing horrible wooden shoes and ripped uniforms, and some with no shoes at all. Also everyone who left Russia had to go through a Disinfectant Station because of lice. A joke made the rounds that Germany was not a civilized country because they had no Disinfection Stations.

POW's who came from the USA were well fed and wore clean clothes and shoes. They had duffle bags full of their belongings. Many Germans came from Silesia, Pommern, what is now Poland. Also Sudeten Gau, which became Czechoslovakia, and from other border countries. The French still recruited men for the Foreign Legion, and was told they fed the German POW's very poorly. They made barbeque in front of the prisoners to make them so hungry that they would sign themselves up for the Foreign Legion.

Many families never found each other even after many years. The Red Cross worked with them and was always searching to bring families together again.

In 1953 I made it to West Berlin. Since so many people arrived daily, we, about 40 girls under 25 years old, were flown from then Templehof Airport in Berlin to Hannover, and from there by bus to Westertimke, near Hannover.

It took about three to four weeks to be processed to receive our West German Passport and to be allowed to stay in the West. Not everybody was that lucky. Some were sent back into the DDR (Deutsch Democratic Republic) if they were found to be spies.

We also received job assignments. Some lucky girls had relatives in West Germany; others were assigned to domestic jobs since they had no other education. I was sent to Koblenz where I was offered a job in their city hospital or another job in Mainz. I chose Mainz. Although Koblenz is a very charming city with much history, I wanted Mainz since it is like a sister city to Wiesbaden. And I liked that area.

I had a very enjoyable week in Koblenz and learned all about the history of the lovely town. During all this time I lived with nuns in a row house and slept in one room with ten beds. I ate and slept there and I was grateful that they gave me my first shelter in West Germany.

I was on my way to Mainz. The *Zahn & Kieferklinik* Tooth and Jaw Clinic was located directly inside the Johannes Gutenberg University and was run by Professor Doctor Hermann.

According to the nurses uphill in the Mainzer City Hospital, I was very lucky to land this job. Our patients were mostly from France, Monaco and German business people with money. Germany was still recovering after that devastated war.

Those were private patients with private rooms, and they did not leave until their dentures were completed. For the first time in my life I realized big money has power. It was not like in East Germany where everybody was poor and the daily life was "fight for what you need." Here the stores were so full of things that I had to get used to it.

With my first monthly pay I wanted to buy myself a pair of good shoes. It was a pleasure to have such a big selection in the stores. I wanted to write about everything to my mother and I hoped she would believe me. From then on I also sent many care packages East. Chocolate, coffee, nonperishables, some old clothes, umbrellas, for instance, were the type of things my family could not get in East Germany. My letters went to the police first, and then they were delivered to my mother.

Now I lived inside the clinic. Some rooms were for patients and the same type of rooms were used for us. I shared with other one nurse, my friend in the office. We were encouraged to take courses in medical fields at the university and we ate in the Mensa (student cafeteria) where all students ate.

"*Fasching time*" (Mardi Gras) was unforgettably crazy and full of irresponsibility. Students hired river boats and cruised up and down the Rhine River. They partied until Ash Wednesday. Then things got back to normal and many people started again to save money for next year's party.

In the clinic, we often fixed broken jaws from motorbike accidents. But most of all older well-to-do people from Monaco and Nizza came to get new dentures because our clinic was known for perfect fits.

I loved that job and enjoyed it all the more because we got more free time than the nurses up the hill in the city hospital. I explored the city of Mainz and the Rhine River, everything was new to me. Every butcher and dry cleaners seemed to be called Emmerich (my maiden name). But they did not want to admit to being related to a poor refugee girl.

The nurses I worked with were mostly also from East Germany. They had come earlier. I made very good friends and I stayed there for several years. Meanwhile the wall went up in East Berlin, and they were shooting their own people who tried to cross. Our newspaper showed us pictures of the people shot.

One day we got an American patient; he was an Army Colonel stationed in Mainz. He was the liveliest and funniest soldier, not at all a stiff person like some of the other patients. I picked up English very well. I had to pay for a class to learn English with some other nurses. People wanted to be able to talk to the Americans. They were glad they were there and that they received American patients too. He always had friends visiting and a few times a real hunk of a man came to visit. His name was Walter and he was a long time friend of our patient. He came often and not only to see the Colonel. After I had

126

some pleasant conversations with him, he asked me out and we started dating.

Walter was a real gentleman. He took me to the best places to eat. At that time, a little outside of town, butcheries had small restaurants with really good food. Mainz and Wiesbaden (sister cities) were also very close so we went out to both. When I had gotten this job, the union had given yellow tickets, and one time there was a show with Hungarian dance groups. Before, Walter hadn't wanted to use my tickets, but then he was fascinated and we started going to shows with my tickets. We also went to gatherings with American families.

For two years we dated and tried to get married, but the paper war was unbelievable. They wanted my mother's marriage certificate from East Germany, for instance. It took us so long. Every time we brought a new document to the American authorities they were asking for something else, in threefold and in both the English and German languages. Only this one translator was acceptable. He had an office with papers stacked to the ceiling. We had to beg him to do our translation. We already had a huge folder of documents together when Walter was transferred to Munich down in Bavaria. It was impossible for me to move there, and I was sure we would never see each other again. I thought everything would fall apart.

But I underestimated the man who was to become my husband. He continued to work on those wedding papers. Walter secured an American apartment in Munich while I still lived in Mainz. Quarters could only be kept for so long or someone else would move in. He made an appointment with the *Standesamt* (Marriage Office for Germans marrying foreigners) in City Hall, and I had to pack my belongings in a jiffy to come to take the train to Munich. I wore whatever I could find and I had no bouquet. I wanted one, so he gave me some marks to go into the flower store. I asked for something green and quick, but she said no, it must be full and nice. Walter was waiting. He had to run for two witnesses and though everyone worked on Tuesday, he found them. Downstairs was the marriage office, and upstairs the judge put on his robe and called people in to get married. They did very it nicely, and even had an organ playing.

Walter was so emotional tears came down his face. He had been so anxious to make things happen so fast. It was the last day for the apartment. And then we went to eat. He started to carry me across the threshold. I didn't know what he wanted. We had put our stuff down and he turned to me. What did he want now? It was so unexpected.

The City of Munich was closed to newcomers, because the city was filled to capacity with refugees. Living space was nowhere to be found. Germany then had a system that any person who wanted to live in Munich had to get permission from the *Einwohnermeldeamt* (Office for Habitants) in the city. I don't think there is a right word in English. They still have a system that when you move from one place to another, you have to fill out a form for the police. It may not be the police now though.

Walter already had work for me waiting. I signed in for the job, working as a teletype operator in an American facility. I transcribed and wrote up letters and paperwork and messages that came in from maneuvers. It was a poking machine that poured out long thin strips of paper from the side. It had to be correct and they were usually in code.

Luckily I knew how to type. It was so different-the work, the life in Munich, and the wedding. It had to be quick because the apartment could not be held any longer. They finally had pity on us and let us get married but not before I had to spend one whole day at the American Embassy for examination. They administered a physical examination to see if I was sick and also a mental exam and saw how much English I spoke.

We suddenly got permission and in Munich we married. We moved into our beautiful new apartment and were finally able to live a normal life together. The wedding was hilariously funny, with witnesses quickly found. We celebrated in a restaurant close to the English Garden. It was truly a whirlwind-wedding, and the apartment was now ours.

My mother was happy to hear the news. We never heard from Volker and his Father had died earlier that year. My brothers got married in East Germany. They had to live their life and I lived mine. Although I searched for my Papa, he never came back and must have died somewhere in Russia. At one time he wrote to us that heavy fighting was going on at the Caucasus mountains because of the oil there. My father, on the other hand I only know he was driving red cross trucks with wounded away from the front. In those days not many people knew how to drive a car. All that luxury came later. Trucks of wounded were also attacked during the war. Father perished and never came back, so we guess that he got killed somewhere on the road. I still sent care packages to my family. I made enough money to save and do this. Also, my husband felt it was a good thing to do. He proposed to me by saying "Marry me, and I'll show you the world."

He meant every word. After enjoying Munich and the annual Oktoberfest, the city, the mountains, and the many lakes, we were transferred to Lawton, Oklahoma. There, I applied for a nursing job in a beautiful new hospital in Lawton. To my surprise, many of the nurses that I met there were German. So many Germans in Oklahoma? What a surprise. I was looking very much forward to working there in my real profession with all those nice people. We were only there for one year. The green cards laid out in the post office in a stack. Walter said you have to fill out your green card, but nobody wanted them. I said what for?

Then my husband got a new assignment, this time in Ethiopia, Africa. We spent three years in Eritrea. His job was communications and he ran a signal tower in the mountains. One time we were invited by the King of Ethiopia, Haile Selassy, to his castle in Massaua and discovered he had all "Made in USA" appliances and furniture. The King of Ethiopia was married to the Queen who made him King through marriage. She died while we were living there.

We enjoyed Africa, and went on safaris and fishing trips. They had huge shrimp. I never ate so many shrimp as I did during those three years. They also had mushrooms as big as a steak that we picked ourselves, had a friend check if they were good, and then fried. The Italian butcherie was so good and there I learned to make a good roast.

We visited schools and gave gifts to Eritrean children. We women were very much involved in helping Eritrean people. The

130

weather was always an even 75, never more than 80 degrees. Winter was the rainy season, and it started every day at the same time.

There were also many beggars. Parents mutilated their children in order to encourage people, mostly foreigners, to give them more money. Nice clothes were not wanted. The nicer the clothes the less pity people had for them. So our gifts were small. I had a permanent beggar who came every day at the same time and same place for food and a few pennies. Children were sold, but it was strictly forbidden in the Army for us to get involved, otherwise I know we would have taken some of those poor children home with us.

We also made, with many other people, a trip to Israel. In those early days Israel did not have a big hotel so we slept in a *kabbutz* (a youth hostel) for two nights, sharing a room. Then we went to Egypt, and I never ate more oranges in my life then in Cairo. Orange juice places were all over Egypt's capital city. Cairo had big wide avenues with orange juice sellers everywhere, and men sitting smoking pipes. We saw the sphinx and pyramids and other marvelous things like that.

There was a story about a wife who went into a shop and disappeared while her husband waited outside. Over a 100 girls disappeared every year in those Arabian countries (they told us later in Paris).

I saw American merchant ships. Young healthy boys, sailors, going with girls of the night into dark places. *No wonder they came back with diseases*, I thought. We learned that merchant marines would often buy a girl from their families for a cow or camel, which the sailor could buy cheap. The American dollar was very high then. They would keep the girl for as long as they were in the harbor, then leave the girl behind. She could not go back home, because she was considered as being married to that merchant marine. The family pride forbade them to take her back, because she belonged to whoever bought her. But he was gone and from then on those girls became the girls of the night. Nobody inspected them for their health.

Americans were liked by the people of Ethiopia and Eritrea, but Italians, who lived there permanently, were often in danger of being killed by the natives. Sometimes they were intercepted going from home to the airport and were killed. But Americans went out to the villages with milk, toys, and food. I even baked cakes. There was a big cemetery for soldiers, one for Italians and one for Ethiopians. Many things happened there, too numerous to mention.

I enjoyed that country and the Red Sea where we spent many weekends. Since Asmara, the town where we lived, was so high in the mountains, the air we breathed was very thin. So we had to leave the mountains once in a while to breathe normal atmosphere. Ethiopia then had wild herds of baboon monkeys. They often crossed the roads and were very protective of their mates and their young, so we kept our distance.

When our time in Ethiopia came to an end, we were assigned immediately to Paris, France. Before our quarters were ready we stayed three months in a hotel, giving me plenty of time to learn all about Paris with the help of Germans who were once soldiers in the Foreign Legion. They showed us the night life in Paris. They were beautiful shows, but too wild for us. We then moved into wonderful quarters, a house beyond the city in Feucherolls, a few miles outside of Versailles.

132

While my husband worked at the Blockhouse, near the Champs Elysees, I explored the city of Paris. I was amazed at how many French people spoke German. At midday I met my husband at the Rue de Marbeuf for lunch and took newly arrived American families for a tour, either to the Sacré Coeur, the Eiffel Tower, the Bois de Boulogne, or wherever they wanted to go. I took them there. We lived right in the block near the George V Hotel. I stood on Champs Elysees and people thought I was a local and took my pictures.

Here I also met former German POW's who had joined the French Legion years before but now lived and worked in Paris. They spoke French very well and worked in the tourist business. They also told us stories, and everybody who fought in the Foreign Legion now received a modest pension from the French government, but only if they stayed in France. If they would go to live in Germany, they would lose that income.

My best friend from Munich came to visit us with her son. Her son and I went up the Eiffel Tower and felt, at the peak, the Tower swaying in the wind. There was real old antique furniture up there in a small place. Although it was off limits to ordinary people, Wolfgang spoke such polished French that the Tower Keeper bowed and allowed us to go up there. I never forgot it, but Wolfgang, my friends' son, spoke to this man and I never knew what was said. I found myself high up at the Eiffel Tower.

Every weekend my husband and I and the many friends we made at the time went up the hill to Sacré Coeur where we found all the international painters on Butte Montmartre. It was a wonderful time. I watched them paint and we bought a paper-cutting of my profile with my glasses by Claude Marin. I still have it. It was close to the hotel where Elizabeth Taylor, Richard Burton and Errol Flynn stayed.

We were in Paris when President Kennedy was assassinated. It was a terrible blow to people and we were very sad. To think that something like that could happen in our modern time.

From Paris we were assigned to Stuttgart, Germany. In 1965 all retirees were allowed to come free from East to West Germany, and my mother came after all those years. She had much, so very much, to tell me. But she also was very ill. In East Germany she was told she had arthritis and had to live with it. In West Germany I took her to a specialist. We were told that she had kidney cancer and would not live very much longer.

Since this was her first visit to West Germany ever, we went to the supermarket, where she saw a mountain of oranges. She said, "They must be phony. They cannot be real." So we bought some. I also wanted her to have a good pair of shoes. She was so astounded that the first store we went in had just the right shoes for her and that when we left the sales girl opened the door for us. Mom was overwhelmed.

Many other things she saw and wondered about. I saw her writing letters to my brothers. I asked, "Are you writing everything you see Mom?"

"Oh no, I cannot," she said. "They would think you brain washed me. They won't believe me."

I was so happy to have my mother with us, and we wanted to take her along to the Good Olde USA, but it was not to be. She passed away while she was with us after only two months.

Now my husband was homesick. Walter had had enough of Europe and wanted to go back to the USA. We were lucky to get tickets on the big USS United States, a ship as big and long as a city block. I had a wonderful time and gained 12 pounds, which I lost rapidly once we were in Pennsylvania where we visited family till our house was ready. We moved into an apartment, an Army place in Prince Georges' County, Maryland.

I loved my husband's family in Pennsylvania. They were such wonderful people and took me in as if I was an American. And I gladly thanked them for it. We made many visits later on when we lived in Maryland, and I enjoyed it and wished we could live there. My husband also inherited some property there that he wanted to use for future plans.

For many years we lived in Maryland where my husband eventually retired, and we bought a newly built house in Gambrills. "Our first house," he said. Later on we would buy a bigger one, we said. It never happened, but we were very happy in our little house and if two people really love each other, they are happy in the smallest hut.

Walter retired from the Army and worked for a while at NASA until he was able to get a government job where he worked until total retirement. Unfortunately, he died in 2009.

Now I am left behind with my dog, a Lab named Rusty. Age wears on me and I no longer use all the ceramic molds in my backyard artisan cottage. Over the years I've enjoyed knitting, macramé, making lace and other crafts which I often give to friends or were used as small table gifts for special occasions. I also treasure the fourteen years I taught German in the local schools and my many years of volunteer work with Army Community Services at Fort George G. Meade

I am still active in our local Lutheran church and sing in the choir. I am also a member of the LA Fitness near my home with a pool, and I continue in the German-American Club near the post. My last battles were not in East Germany and included a fight against breast cancer which I overcame several years ago.

***

I began writing these pages nearly twenty years ago. The memories of my life in Germany before World War Two, the fear after the war, my dangerous crossings into West Germany and my life under the oppressive Communists are as vivid and real today as ever.

It is said that everyone has a story and this is part of mine. People tell me it is remarkable, and maybe it is, but I know it is not unique. Millions of people were caught behind the Iron Curtain against their will and suffered terribly. Countless thousands died senselessly and tragically. I came close to dying many times. The only reason I escaped was because of the kindness of others and the protection of God.

Freedom is a different sort of thing. When you have it and grow up with it, it might be the last thing you think about. When you don't, it seems as far away as a dream. I am thankful for the freedom I have and the country that has opened its arms to me and allowed me to enjoy that freedom. I also remember enjoying freedom as a small child in Germany before the Nazis took over. We should never take freedom for granted because it can disappear so very quickly if we let it.

I have lived in many places in my life. Some were places of hiding and others of comfort. Dwellings filled with fear and those of love, a refuge from what is dark and evil. All my life I strive for my home. A place without tears or sorrow or pain. I have not found it yet.

Soon a day will come when I will leave this world as we all must. On that wonderful day I will meet my Jesus and see my beloved Walter again. On that day I will feel the arms of my mother around me. On that day I will weep in joy to see all those lost and yet alive again.

On that day, I will finally, after all this time, be home.

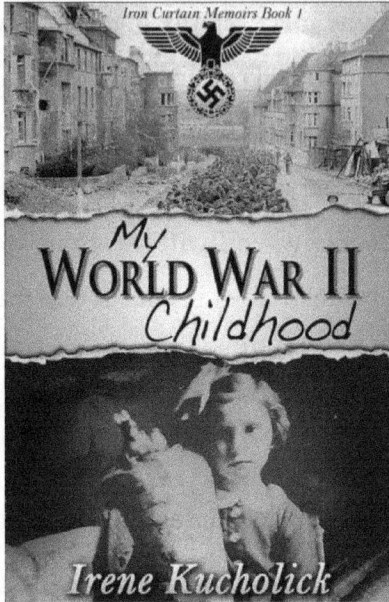

Iron Curtain Memoirs Book 1

My WORLD WAR II Childhood

Irene Kucholick

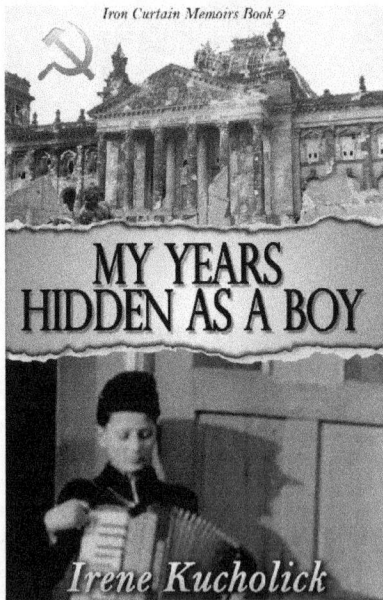

Iron Curtain Memoirs Book 2

MY YEARS HIDDEN AS A BOY

Irene Kucholick

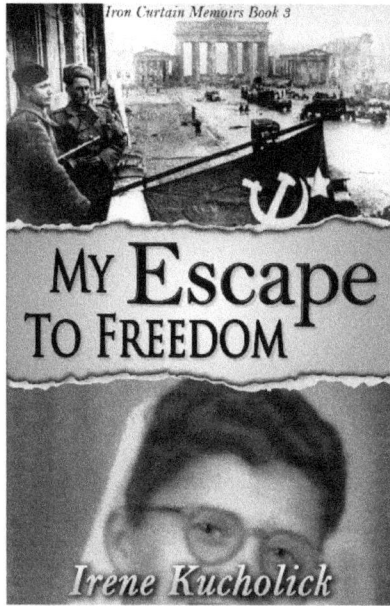

Iron Curtain Memoirs Book 3

My Escape
To Freedom

Irene Kucholick

Get all 3 in 1 book.

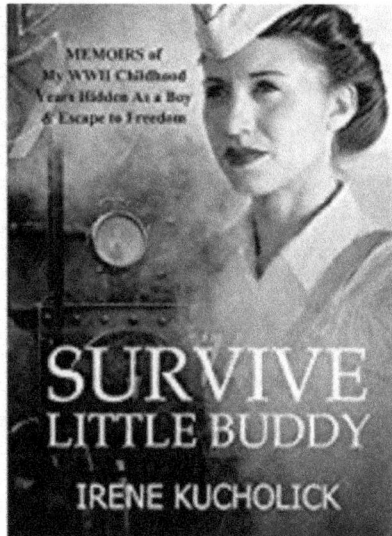

MEMOIRS of
My WWII Childhood
Years Hidden As a Boy
& Escape to Freedom

SURVIVE
LITTLE BUDDY

IRENE KUCHOLICK

www.ingramcontent.com/pod-product-compliance
Lightning Source LLC
Chambersburg PA
CBHW031534040426
42445CB00010B/538